Mrs. Crudlen & I

A NOVEL APPROACH TO BASIC ANATOMY AND PHYSIOLOGY

Mimi Mathis

Mrs. Crudlen & I
A Novel Approach to Basic Anatomy and Physiology

The material and information in this book are for general information, entertainment, and self-care purposes only. The material and information do not substitute for professional medical advice. If readers need medical advice, they should consult a doctor or other appropriate medical professional.

The author/publisher does not assume and hereby disclaim any liability to any party for any loss, damage, or disruption caused by errors or omissions, whether such errors or omissions result from negligence, accident, or any other cause.

This book was created with the assistance of AI. It is not meant to be used as an official A&P textbook

Author and Publisher: Mimi Mathis
mimimartinauthor@gmail.com

Dedicated to the Reader

Table of Contents

CHAPTER 1
Mrs. Crudlen & I

Mrs. Crudlen is a remarkable ninety-year-old gray-headed lady whose presence commands attention and respect. The many deep wrinkles on her face tell a meaningful, captivating story of a life filled with wisdom, memories, tough times, and strength. Her beautiful, layered haircut frames her wrinkled face. The strands of her gray hair retain a certain shine that reflects her vitality and is a testament to her enduring spirit and the many tales she could tell. Mrs. Crudlen's blue eyes are truly mesmerizing. They sparkle and gleam with the love of life, speaking volumes without uttering a single word.

Despite her advanced age, Mrs. Crudlen exudes an aura of strength and resilience. She walks with a slight limp and carries herself with quiet dignity and grace, her every movement deliberate and meaningful.

In addition to her striking physical presence, Mrs. Crudlen possesses brain superpowers that leave those around her in awe. Her extraordinary mental abilities make her mind sharp and agile, capable of feats that defy her age. Her cognitive skills are unmatched, allowing her to solve complex problems, recall details from decades past, and understand intricate concepts with ease, especially about the miraculous human body.

Mrs. Crudlen lives alone, still drives her car, and loves to time travel and spread her knowledge and love wherever she goes. With a sharp mind and keen intuition, she astounds those around her with her ability to teach basic Anatomy and Physiology while inspiring people to take care of their bodies. Her humor and jokes occasionally push the boundaries of good taste, but there is no denying her irresistible charisma, which draws people to her.

Mrs. Crudlen is a living legend, and a beacon of strength and intelligence, proving that age is just a number, and the power of the mind is infinite.

Meet Mimi

My name is Mimi Mathis. I met Mrs. Crudlen many years ago when I taught Anatomy and Physiology for Licensed Practical Nurses. I also have gray hair, but mine is unruly and lacks luster, and my saggy, time-worn face is adorned with countless deep wrinkles. I love my family, animals, music, and writing. During my nursing career, I enjoyed home health, management, and teaching. I especially loved Geriatrics—and now I'm one!

Despite my physical changes and the struggles that come with growing older, my spirit remains unbroken. I have a healthy imagination and a genuine desire to help others enjoy reading about Anatomy and Physiology and gain an understanding of their bodies that goes beyond just memorizing facts. Most of all, I want everyone to cherish and take care of their bodies. That is the main reason for writing about Anatomy and Physiology, or A&P, which is the accepted abbreviation for Anatomy and Physiology.

In addition to reviewing basic Uh-nat-uh-me and Fiz-ee-ol-uh-jee, the book will include a few common basic medical terms. The first two terms are anatomy and physiology. Anatomy is the body's structure, and physiology is how the living body works.

***

One gorgeous summer day, I called Mrs. Crudlen and asked if she would help me write this book. I told her I had lost my self-confidence and didn't think I could write it without her help. Her response was immediate.

"Mimi Mathis, I certainly would like to help you! Can you come over this afternoon at 1:00? If you recall, I live at 123 Memory Lane."

"Yes ma'am! I will be there! I am honored that you will help me. I remember where Memory Lane is located. I will see you soon. Thank you! Bye."

"Bye. I'll see you when I see you," she replied with a soft giggle that infused her words with a touch of amusement before hanging up the phone.

My heart was aflutter with anticipation. I could hardly contain my excitement driving down Memory Lane to her tiny house. The road was lined with vibrant wildflowers swaying gently in the breeze, their colors dancing in the sunlight. Majestic oak trees whispered stories of the past as their branches reached out to caress the sky. The golden rays of the sun cast a nostalgic haze over everything I passed. Each moment filled my heart with a longing to be with my husband Jack, and our three sons, Sean, Shannon, and Shea. This drive was a journey through time, where every moment echoed with laughter, tears, and the sweet embrace of cherished memories.

When I arrived at 123 Memory Lane, I cleared my mind of the past, parked in the driveway, and saw an older woman standing on the front porch. I thought it was Mrs. Crudlen, but I wasn't sure. I quickly got out of the car, walked toward the porch, waved, and yelled, "Is your name Mrs. Crudlen?"

"If you are not the FBI it is!" she yelled back.

It took me a few seconds to realize that was indeed Mrs. Crudlen. Her strange and funny humor gave her away. I laughed as I hobbled up the porch. She greeted me with a warm smile and loving hug. Next, she poured me a large glass of water and sat it on a small table between two wooden rocking chairs.

We sat in the rocking chairs, started rocking, sipping water, and enjoyed being together.

A minute later, Mrs. Crudlen stopped rocking and looked at me. "Mimi, before we get started on reviewing Anatomy and Physiology, I want to talk to you about what you told me over the phone."

"What is it?" I asked with a desire to hear more, looking her straight in the eyes.

"You told me that you lost your self-confidence and did not think you could write your book without my help. Lack of confidence can foster negative thought patterns and self-doubt that can lead to a cycle of negative thinking, where your brain becomes conditioned to focus on failures and shortcomings. Start visualizing yourself succeeding in various scenarios. This mental rehearsal can help reduce anxiety, increase confidence in real-life situations, and remind yourself of your strengths and past successes. Lack of self-confidence can significantly impact both your brain function and overall performance."

Her eyes widened slightly with a harsh intensity in her gaze. "Mimi Mathis, if you think you can't—you can't!"

Next, her eyes began to sparkle with kindness and her lips curved into one of the sweetest smiles I had ever seen.

I immediately responded to her smile. "I can write about basic Anatomy and Physiology! I'm sorry I said I lost my self-confidence."

"Mimi, you do not need to be sorry. Be thankful you can learn and do things. And remember that sorry is as sorry does. Saying sorry is important, but it is equally important to show you truly mean it through your actions."

Mrs. Crudlen was right again. I smiled as a sense of ease washed over me. "Thank you for your words. My actions will be that I'll work hard on this project. Where do I start?"

"You need to start with your prefrontal cortex in your brain to help you stay focused, set goals, and assess your progress, which in turn boosts your confidence." She paused, folded her wrinkled hands in her lap, and said, "I think it would be a good idea to have everyone who reads the book use their bodies and imagination to help them understand basic A & P. In addition to that, there is a lot of other information on the internet about A&P. Before you came today, I researched the internet and found hundreds of outstanding educational websites with tutorials and flashcards. And there are hundreds of incredible resources on YouTube videos."

Next, her brows furrowed, and there was an intense focus in her eyes, like someone deep in thought. Then, she said, loud and clear, "By the time I finished my internet search, I was exhausted and understood why they call that blinking light on the screen a cursor!"

I burst out laughing as Mrs. Crudlen uplifted my spirit with her cursor statement. I could hardly wait to hear what was next. After I stopped laughing, and a few seconds of total silence, she asked, "Mimi, can you name all eleven of the human body organ systems?"

"Yes, ma'am. After all these years, I can because of Mrs. Crudlen & I."

"Good. Let me hear them."

"Here goes! ***Mrs. Crudlen & I***   **M** for Muscular

R for Respiratory   **S** for Skeletal   **C** for Circulatory

R for Reproductive   **U** for Urinary   **D** for Digestive

L for Lymphatic   **E** for Endocrine   **N** for Nervous

I for Integumentary."

I quickly remembered the eleven body organ systems thanks to Mrs. Crudlen & I.

Remembering and reciting the eleven organ systems gave me a burst of energy. However, when I looked at Mrs. Crudlen, she had a serious look on her face with a silent power that told me she had something important to tell me. I resisted the urge to let my mind wander back to the systems and gave her my undivided attention.

"Mimi, understanding about the human body is one of the most valuable things anyone can ever learn. The human body is phenomenal. And much of what it does is without conscious effort on our part. Everything our body does is unmatched in its complexity and worth. All the high technology in the world does not compare with our bodies. Besides that, every remarkable machine, including Artificial Intelligence, would not exist or have any value without the human to invent it and use it. Understanding basic anatomy and physiology can unlock a deeper comprehension of how the body works and develop gratitude for all it does for us. This knowledge empowers us to honor our bodies and take care of them in the best possible way while making the right decisions about nutrition, exercise, sleep, managing stress, and overall wellness. Humans are complex physical, emotional, social, and spiritual beings. Wouldn't it be wonderful if more people would take better care of themselves, love themselves and others more, and forgive themselves and others?" She paused, smiled, and then said, "Move over Marvel Legends! After reading your book, more human superheroes are on the way!"

She paused again, her eyes narrowed with a genuine and concerned look. "Now, I want to tell you something near and dear to my heart related to the human body and Earth. It is essential and needs to be in the book."

"What is it?" I asked with great curiosity.

"Before I tell you, I would like you to look at the sky and look at my yard and then tell me what you see."

I quickly replied "Okay" and told her what I saw. "I see fluffy white clouds floating above in the beautiful blue sky. The sun is shining so bright it makes me feel like I'm shining too. The sunbeams are casting a warm glow over the beautiful old oak, pine trees, green grass, and colorful, blooming flowers….it's captivating." I paused and put my hand on my heart. "Everything feels peaceful and looks alive; it soothes my soul and fills me with wonder."

"Good for you, Mimi. That was nice. It sounds like you appreciate Planet Earth." She paused and I noticed a sparkle in her eyes, followed by a gentle smile. "That is what is near and dear to my heart that I wanted to tell you; humans are interconnected to our planet, Earth. We have a profound impact on the earth. The air we breathe and the food we eat come from the Earth. Taking care of Earth means taking care of ourselves."

I nodded in agreement and smiled.

"Now, close your eyes and take some deep breaths to calm your mind and use your imagination."

I closed my eyes, took deep breaths, relaxed, and she began talking.

"Mimi, picture the vast expanse of the ocean stretching out before you, with shades of blue water as far as the eye can see. Visualize the sunlight dancing on the surface of the water as the waves gracefully caress the sandy beach with a gentle lapping sound, creating a soothing melody as they break against the shore and release energy. Do you feel a sense of peace and serenity wash over you as you connect with the image of the beauty and power of the ocean?"

"Yes, I do. I love going to the ocean. It makes me feel connected to Earth," I quickly responded.

"Good. Now dive into the wonder of Earth being about 70% water, and your body being around 62% water. Your brain is approximately 75% water, blood 83%, heart 79%, bones 22%, muscles 75%, liver 86%, and kidneys 83%. If those numbers do not convince the reader to drink water, I do not know what will?"

"Wow! I'm convinced! I'm so glad you reminded me! That's why it is so important to drink enough water and other beneficial fluids each day to keep healthy." I paused, picked up the glass of water, and drank some large gulps.

Mrs. Crudlen smiled. "In general, humans will not survive over three days without water. Besides water, the balance of oxygen in our bodies mirrors its presence on Earth. Humans can only live a few minutes without oxygen."

A more serious look suddenly appeared on Mrs. Crudlen's face as she pointed to a huge oak tree in her yard. Standing tall and majestic, its branches were filled with rich green leaves fluttering in the breeze. Its sturdy, large trunk with its rough weathered bark was a testament to the tree's resilience and endurance.

CHAPTER 2
The Old Oak Tree

"Mimi, that beautiful old oak is probably 150 years old. Trees are extraordinary living organisms that play a vital role in maintaining the health of Earth and the well-being of its inhabitants, including humans. I would like you to use your imagination and let us talk with this Old Oak."

I grinned and nodded, and the conversation began.

"Hello, Old Oak. It is a lovely day, isn't it?" Mrs. Crudlen asked.

"Ah, it is indeed. The sun is warm, and the breeze is gentle. How can I assist you today, nice lady?" His voice filled with the richness of a life well-lived and the authority of someone who has weathered countless storms.

"I know trees do a lot for our planet. Would you be so kind as to tell my younger friend how you do that?"

"I certainly will," replied Old Oak. "Younger Friend, trees play many crucial roles. During the process of photosynthesis, we take in carbon dioxide and produce and release oxygen. A single mature tree can produce enough oxygen for up to four people every day. This process also helps by storing carbon in our trunks, branches, and roots." There was a hint of gravel in his voice, a testament to the battles fought and hardships overcome. "Beyond oxygen production, trees also act as natural air filters. We remove dust, pollen, and other pollutants from the air and trap them on our leaves and bark. Urban areas with more trees tend to have better air quality, making them healthier places to live. We give shade and can cool cities by up to 10 degrees." His voice was deep and resonant, carrying the weight of over a century's worth of experience and wisdom.

"That is incredibly important. Please tell us what else you do," Mrs. Crudlen said.

"Our roots help prevent soil erosion by holding the soil in place. This improves soil structure and reduces water runoff. By reducing runoff, we also prevent water pollution and reduce the risk of landslides and flooding. We also enhance soil fertility by contributing organic matter as our leaves and branches decompose. Our roots absorb and store rainwater, which helps to replenish groundwater supplies." There was a deliberate slowness to his speech, each word carefully chosen and imbued with the richness of a lifetime of knowledge.

"We are fun to climb, swing on, sit under, and use in fireplaces in the winter. We provide habitats for countless creatures. Birds nest in our branches, insects live in our bark, and even mammals find shelter and food among our leaves and roots. We protect and ensure the survival of many endangered species." Suddenly, his voice began to rumble like distant thunder. "But careless humans are preventing us from doing our job for innocent creatures because they are destroying us with fires! Humans cause 80 to 90% of all wildfires!"

"I'm so sorry," I blurted out.

"Thank you, Younger Friend. I do not think the idiots who started the fires know that trees have a great impact on their lives."

Tears flooded my eyes. I walked under the shade of the old oak tree, and its huge, old branches stretched out like protective arms, offering solace and shelter. I leaned on the tree, and my tears vanished.

"Old Oak, you are a symbol of strength, longevity, and connection to the natural world. Every word you said will be in my book! Thank you!"

"You're welcome, Younger Friend. Remember, together, we can ensure a healthier planet for all living beings." He paused. I stepped back, and he said, "By the way, Planet Earth has been here for over 4 billion years. It is not going anywhere—we are!" His leaves fluttered in the breeze like he was waving goodbye to me. "It is time for you to go now. Mrs. Crudlen is waiting for you."

When I reached over and touched Old Oak, I felt the rough bark against my skin and the subtle vibrations of his life force. Tears flooded my eyes again. I knew I had just exchanged energy with this incredible ancient being.

I turned around, and the second I walked back to Mrs. Crudlen, she started talking. "Mimi, studies have shown that spending time in nature reduces stress, improves mood and sleep, and promotes physical activity. How wonderful it would be if more people would plant a tree!"

After Mrs. Crudlen stopped talking, she bent down, took off her shoes and socks, stood up, and walked across the yard and back, barefooted on the green grass. Suddenly, her eyes shined bright with a captivating sparkle. "Science has proven that humans are made from the most common elements found on and in Earth. There are many ways to connect with nature. What physiological capabilities do you have that enable you to perceive and interact with the world around you, including Mother Nature?"

"Uh-uh-uh," I stuttered. My eyes darted around as I grappled with what I thought was a puzzling question. To hide my emotions, I took a long, deep breath and let it out. Then, for some unknown reason, I lowered my head and placed my open hand in the center of my forehead and saw that my wide-toed tennis shoe was untied. That did it! Touching my forehead and seeing my shoe reminded me that touch and sight are two of our main senses, or physiological capabilities, as she called them. "Touch and sight!" I exclaimed. Next, I touched my nose and said, "Smell." Then, I pointed to my mouth with my forefinger and said, "Taste." Finally, I shifted my finger to my ear and said, "Hearing."

"Good! Touch, sight, smell, taste, and hearing, better known as the five primary senses, enable us to perceive and interact meaningfully with the world around us. Touch is also called tactile. The brain processes the information received from these senses to form a clear understanding of what is going on, enabling us to react and adapt to various situations effectively. Overall, human senses are important for survival, communication, and for experiencing the good times, and the tough times in life."

She paused and smiled. "And do not forget that there is another sense in humans, often referred to as intuition, which is the ability to perceive information beyond the five physical senses. It is the gut feeling or instinct that guides us in decision-making and helps us sense things that cannot be explained logically. I think that little children use their intuition a lot, and then as they grow, they stop using it as often. But with practice and openness, people can harness this powerful tool to navigate through life with more clarity and confidence."

"I have a gut feeling you are right!" I blurted out. "Thank you for your knowledge and this conversation. I've enjoyed every minute of it." I leaned back and started rocking, and Mrs. Crudlen began rocking.

We rocked in unison for a minute, when suddenly she stopped and said, "It is time to move on to basic Anatomy and Physiology. For instance, did you know that using the rocking chair primarily engages the muscles in the lower body and core? The main muscles used are the quadriceps in the thighs, which help to extend and straighten the legs as you push the chair forward. The calf muscles also play a role in providing power for the rocking motion. Additionally, the muscles in the buttocks and hips, such as the gluteus maximus and hip flexors, are activated to stabilize and propel the body while rocking. The core muscles, including the abdominals and lower back muscles, help to maintain balance and support the rocking movement."

I stopped rocking, drank some more water, and hoped she wouldn't ask me to repeat what she just said.

Mrs. Crudlen smirked like she knew intuitively what I was thinking, picked up her glass, took a sip of water, made a soft, muffled "thhhh" sound, and said, "We are within spitting distance of talking about the study of the anatomy of cells and tissues in the body. But before we go there, the reader needs to be reminded that humans are the most complicated species on our planet and our entire body is made of atoms."

I instantly responded with a great big smile.

"Mimi Mathis, you certainly have a bright and contagious smile. Did you know a bright smile is not just a facial expression; it is a reflection of the brain's activity? When you smile, your brain releases neurotransmitters like dopamine, which contribute to feelings of happiness and well-being. Additionally, the act of smiling triggers activity in the brain's amygdala, which processes positive emotions. This neural response to smiling can improve your mood, reduce stress levels, strengthen your immune system, and enhance your ability to connect with others. So, next time you flash a bright smile, remember that it is not just your face lighting up, but your brain generating joy and harmony within and to those around you." Mrs. Crudlen winked at me and smiled.

I didn't say a word. I just kept smiling big.

All of a sudden, Mrs. Crudlen's face lit up with another bright smile as a sparkle of excitement danced in her eyes. "I just retrieved some valuable information from my hippocampus, prefrontal cortex, and the amygdala in my brain's temporal lobe that contribute to the encoding and retrieval of memories related to reading and acquiring knowledge. The information is that we need to add a little chemistry to the book! The study of chemistry is unlocking the mysteries of how our bodies work on a molecular level. Body functions depend on cellular functions, and cellular functions result from chemical change."

CHAPTER 3
Chemistry of Life

"Mrs. Crudlen, the only thing I remember about Chemistry is that it is a branch of science that deals with the composition, structure, and properties of substances and the changes they go through."

"Do not worry about it. You do not have to be a Rocket Surgeon to understand what I will tell you."

"Rocket Surgeon?" My mind darted around, searching for clarity about a Rocket Surgeon. Then, I started laughing. "That's funny. I remember Foghorn Leghorn saying Rocket Surgeon on Looney Tunes years ago, but I don't remember what he meant to say."

"I will be right back. While I am gone, think about the hippocampus in your brain sending the Rocket Surgeon memory to the cortex in your brain to be stored as a long-term memory. You can do it!"

When I shut my eyes and focused on the memory, the words Rocket Scientist flashed in my mind. Foghorn Leghorn meant to say Scientist not Surgeon!

I began laughing, and when I opened my eyes, Mrs. Crudlen stood before me, wearing a knee-length pristine white lab coat.

Her crisp lab coat contrasted sharply with her deeply wrinkled yet vibrant face. Her grey hair was pulled back into a tight bun on top of her head, giving her an air of authority. She had transformed into Professor Crudlen, a retired chemistry professor who still found joy in teaching, even in her golden years.

Professor Crudlen adjusted her dark-rimmed glasses and smiled warmly at me. "Chemistry, my dear, is the study of matter and how it changes. Everything around us is made up of matter—solids, liquids, and gases. All matter is made of atoms. The two basic ingredients, or components, in the Universe are matter and energy. Energy is the ability to do work or create change. But now, I want to focus on how chemistry relates to the human body, which is a marvel of chemistry itself. I will talk about atoms, molecules, and compounds."

She reached into her pocket and pulled out a miniature model of an atom—a plastic ball with smaller balls attached by thin rods. "This is a simple model of an atom. The ball in the center is the nucleus, and it contains protons and neutrons. The smaller balls orbiting around it are electrons. Atoms are the tiny building blocks of everything. A stack of 1,000,000 atoms would be the same thickness as a sheet of paper. The human body is composed of about 7 octillion atoms. That would be the number 7 followed by 27 zeros! Next, she began swinging the atom back and forth on the string with a slow, rhythmic movement that captured my attention. It calmed me and put me in heightened focus and suggestibility. Then, she smiled and put the atom in her pocket.

"Atoms are the building blocks of matter, and they combine to form molecules in the body. Molecules are made up of two or more atoms bonded together. The average human body is made up of trillions of molecules. Elements are substances that consist of only one type of atom, such as oxygen, carbon, and hydrogen. These elements are essential for the body's functions, like oxygen for respiration and carbon for energy production. Compounds are substances made up of two or more different elements, like water, H_2O, or glucose, $C_6H_{12}O_6$. Compounds are vital for the body as structural components. Examples are enzymes and hormones. Overall, atoms, molecules, elements, and compounds work together in the body to maintain vital functions and support life processes."

She smiled. "Now I will mention some of the elements that make up our bodies—oxygen, carbon, hydrogen, and nitrogen. Oxygen is crucial for respiration. Carbon forms the structure of all our biomolecules—proteins, carbohydrates, fats, and nucleic acids.

"Hydrogen," she continued, "is found in nearly every molecule in the body, including water, and plays a vital role in energy production and maintaining the pH balance of our blood. pH stands for potential of hydrogen. It is a measure of the acidity or alkalinity of a solution. The scale ranges from zero, the most acidic, to 14, the most alkaline. A healthy balance is around 7.35-7.45, which is slightly alkaline. If the pH balance is off, it can lead to health issues.

"And nitrogen," she added, "is a key component of amino acids, the building blocks of proteins. Without nitrogen, we would not be able to grow, repair tissues, or reproduce."

Professor Crudlen paused, her right hand sweeping across the air, "The body is a marvel of chemistry. Atoms and molecules combine to create elements, which combine to form the compounds that sustain life. With each breath you take, every drop of water you drink, and every bite of food you eat, chemistry is at work, ensuring your body functions perfectly."

It was clear that Professor Crudlen enjoyed the fascination of Chemistry. She was indeed in her element, and I wasn't surprised when she asked, "Would you like to hear the composition of the elements in the human body?"

"I would love to!" I quickly responded.

Suddenly, Mrs. Crudlen's words tumbled out in a rush of enthusiasm with a beautiful tone and enchanting rhythm. "In your body there is 62% water, 65% oxygen, 18% carbon, 9.5% hydrogen, 3.2% nitrogen, 1.5% calcium, 1.2% phosphorus, 0.4% potassium, 0.2 % sulfur, 0.2% sodium, 0.2% chlorine, 0.1% magnesium, 16% protein, 1% carbohydrate, 16% fat, 6% minerals, and others are less than 1%." Her voice sounded like a seasoned, knowledgeable professor. Her tone brought every element to life. And I relished every moment of it.

"That was incredible! And you sounded amazing!" I exclaimed.

"Thank you. Every human body is amazing. We may look different, but we are all human!"

As the lesson wrapped up, Professor Crudlen gave me a reassuring pat on the hand. "Chemistry can be complex, but it's a fascinating story of how tiny things come together to create something wonderful."

I enjoyed every word and gained a new appreciation for chemistry. I realized that it wasn't just about formulas and equations but about understanding the very essence of life itself.

CHAPTER 4

Cells

"Cells are the miraculous living building blocks of the body. The number of cells in our bodies is trillions and trillions. Maybe around 100 trillion! There are many sizes of cells, but typically cells are so small that they measure 10 to 30 micrometers in diameter." Mrs. Crudlen's eyes sparkled brighter when she asked me. "Do you know exactly how small that is, Mimi?"

"Not exactly, but it is very tiny," I replied softly, wishing I knew the exact answer.

"To put this into perspective, a human's hair is about 100 micrometers wide, so a human cell is about one-tenth the width of fine hair, and that's finer than frog hair split many ways. Our cells are remarkably resilient and versatile, essential for sustaining life and enabling us to thrive."

Her words acted like a bolt of inspiration, wanting me to hear more about human cells. Then she jarred my memory when she said, "The human cell is the basic structural and functional unit of the human body. Human cells communicate with one another, allowing them to coordinate and work together for the body. It is almost beyond my comprehension, and it is a hidden treasure in the most unexpected place – right inside of us."

Next, Mrs. Crudlen raised her glass of water, requested I do the same and made a toast to the human cells. The clinking of our glasses resonated like a harmonious symphony, a small gesture with a significant impact. After we drank some water, she said, "Our body has many types of cells that constantly interact and work together to ensure the proper functioning of our body. They are busy providing structure for the body, taking in food for fuel, getting rid of waste, and reproducing. Cells contain the body's hereditary material. They also allow the transport of different substances and facilitate growth. They adapt to environmental changes, respond to other stimuli, and repair damaged tissues. They are healing machines! Cells vary in size, shape, and function. Cells work together to form tissues, organs, and organ systems. There are different types of cells, but it is the similarities that we will focus on before discussing specialized cells."

I watched with curiosity as Mrs. Crudlen held out her right hand, and with the distal end of her index finger moving at almost warp speed, she said, "Use your brain's intricate networks that enable us to explore new possibilities and envision supernatural realities through the power of your mind and belief. Are you ready, Mimi Mathis?"

"Yes, I am!"

"Good! I call it a sacred journey of self-discovery and enlightenment about your own body."

I took a deep breath, closed my eyes, and heard Mrs. Crudlen's voice vibrate with strength and power. "Welcome, Mimi," she said, her voice echoing, "welcome to the inside of a human cell."

I gasped and found myself floating inside a dazzling, glowing landscape. Suddenly, I was surrounded by a shimmering bubble— the cell membrane.

"This is the cell's protective gate," explained Mrs. Crudlen. "It is a thin, but tough flexible barrier that surrounds all cells. It allows useful substances to enter the cell and blocks the entry of harmful substances. It regulates the flow of nutrients, water, and waste, ensuring the cell's survival. It is a dynamic structure composed of a double layer of fatty compounds, called lipids, interspersed with proteins, acting as both guardian and communicator with the cell's environment.

"The membrane also forces out waste products. Cilia, small hair-like structures located on the outside of most membranes, help with movement and sensory functions," she said.

Next, we drifted further inside, through a gooey, gel-like substance that filled the space. "This is the cytoplasm," she said, scooping a bit of it up with a glowing finger. "It is like the bustling city streets where all the action happens. It holds everything together."

In the distance, we saw a massive, glowing sphere—like a palace. "That is the nucleus, the command center. Inside it lies one of the greatest treasures of all—DNA, Deoxyribonucleic Acid, which holds all our genetic information. It is a blueprint that holds the instructions for building humans and everything we are. DNA is a fascinating molecule that contains a hereditary genetic code that is unique to every individual. It determines an individual's traits and characteristics. I have heard that if you stretched out your DNA, it could reach the sun and back at least three times." She smiled a sunny smile.

We peeked inside the nucleus and saw a shimmering spiral staircase twisting upward. "This," said Mrs. Crudlen proudly, "is DNA, the code of life."

Tiny figures called Chromosomes were zipping up and down the spiral, reading from the ladder's rungs. "Chromosomes are long, thread-like organized structures of DNA and protein found in the nucleus of cells. Chromosomes organize and package the DNA tightly so it can fit inside the cell. During cell division, the chromosomes ensure that each new cell receives the correct amount of genetic material in the form of genes. Each chromosome can contain hundreds to thousands of genes. Genes are the basic units of heredity and are passed from parents to offspring. Each gene has a different job and provides the code to build a particular protein that will have a specific role in the body, such as determining eye color or blood type.

"Humans have 46 chromosomes, arranged in 23 pairs. One set of 23 chromosomes comes from the mother, and the other set comes from the father. Each chromosome is made up of a single DNA molecule that is tightly coiled many times around proteins called histones that support its structure.

"To sum it up, DNA is the complete set of instructions for building and operating a human body. Chromosomes are the organized packages of DNA that make sure these instructions are properly divided and passed on during cell division. Genes are specific instructions within DNA that tell your body how to make proteins and control traits such as eye color.

"Also, the nucleolus is inside the nucleus. It makes ribosomes, which are responsible for protein production.

"Surrounding the nucleus are various specialized structures, called organelles, each with a specific and vital function."

We drifted out of the nucleus and found ourselves near organelles assembling something. "There are the ribosomes," she said. "They read messages from the DNA and build proteins that perform countless tasks, from building cellular structures to facilitating chemical reactions. Another organelle is RNA or ribonucleic acid. It is found in many cell parts and is crucial in protein production. RNA also acts as a messenger to ribosomes, ensuring that the instructions encoded in DNA are properly executed."

She pointed to a busy pathway beside us resembling crocheted lace layers of membranes. "That is the rough and smooth endoplasmic reticulum, called ER. Their purpose is to produce proteins, carbohydrates, and fats for the cell, transport intracellular molecules, store calcium, and help detoxify." She stopped talking and pointed to another busy area.

I watched in wonder as proteins were packed into neat little parcels and sent along winding tubes. "This," she said with a grand gesture, "is the Golgi apparatus, often called the post office of the cell. It helps process and transport molecules within the cell. The Golgi apparatus prepares proteins, and lipids, which are fat molecules, for use in other places inside and outside the cell and sends them where needed. Without it, our cells would be in chaos."

Then, we arrived at what looked like a glowing power station—mitochondria. "Ah, the powerhouse! One of my favorites. These beauties turn food into ATP, adenosine triphosphate which produces energy and supports the immune system in fighting infections. ATP fuels every activity in the cell, from muscle contraction to nerve impulse transmission. Without mitochondria, life would come to a standstill. They are heroes, constantly churning out energy," Mrs. Crudlen proudly announced.

But not everything was peaceful. We noticed odd, blob-like structures prowling around, gobbling up debris. "Those are lysosomes and peroxisomes," she said with a wink. "Lysosomes and peroxisomes are the cell's recycling centers, breaking down and digesting food particles and digesting worn-out cells. They contain enzymes that break down waste materials and cellular debris. They ensure that the cell remains clean and efficient thus preventing damage. They are like garbage collectors."

Suddenly, the shimmering world around us began to fade, and we found ourselves back in the cozy rocking chairs.

"It is incredible," Mrs. Crudlen said softly, "cells work together to keep us alive, healthy, and full of energy. They obtain nutrients and other essential substances from the surrounding body fluids in the spaces around the cells. This fluid is vital in maintaining the balance of chemicals, fluids, and essential nutrients within the body's tissues. Cells can use these nutrients to make the molecules they need to survive, dispose of their waste, maintain their shape and integrity, and reproduce themselves.

"The interplay between the nucleus, organelles, and the cell membrane is a symphony of biological engineering, working in exquisite harmony, and a testament to the elegance of life at the most fundamental level. And there is still so much more to discover and understand about cells and the human body." Her words resonated with an undeniable strength that vibrated through the air.

At that moment, it was as if a gentle light was surrounding me. My mind buzzed with the magic inside me, and I blurted out, "Mrs. Crudlen, this brief journey of a cell has strengthened my respect and gratitude for the gift of life!"

"Mimi, I hope each reader will also honor the delicate dance of life at the cellular level. Remember, when you value your cells, you are valuing your very essence. Showing gratitude for your body can lead to improved self-esteem, mental well-being, and overall health, as well as fostering self-love and providing healing."

Without thinking, I closed my eyes, placed my right hand on my heart, and felt extremely grateful for the trillions and trillions of cells in my body. When I opened my eyes, I noticed Mrs. Crudlen had a bright smile of approval.

Next, we drank some water, and she resumed talking. "Our body has about two hundred different types of cells. These vary in size, shape, and function. Despite their diversity, all cells share common features such as a cell membrane, nucleus, and organelles. Cells depend on each other to keep the body functioning, and each type of cell in the human body is specially equipped for its role. Cells of the same type make up tissues, tissues make up organs, and organs form systems.

"I think it would be fun to review some of the most common types of cells. What do you think, Mimi?"

"I think it would be fun, too." Then with a sense of self-importance and a desire to be recognized by Mrs. Crudlen, I blurted out, "And I think it would also be wonderful if my book inspires readers to become a Cell Biologist to unlock the mysteries of cells that lead to breakthroughs in diseases, treatment, genetic engineering, and improve human health around the world."

She immediately responded, "That sounds great, Mimi. I read the exact words on the internet about Cell Biologists unlocking the mysteries of cells."

I lowered my head and replied, "Small world isn't it."

She grinned, placed her arms across her chest, and said, "Our cells are fascinating! Those crucial little critters are vital to life! Now let us talk about the most common types of cells starting with blood cells.

"Blood cells bring oxygen and nutrients to every cell in our bodies and fight infections. They also pick up cell waste and carry it to your lungs and kidneys to get rid of it. Blood cells are produced by bone marrow found in our bones. The three major types of cells in the blood are red blood cells, white blood cells, and platelets.

"Red blood cells, also called erythrocytes, contain hemoglobin, a protein that gives blood its red color and carries oxygen. A healthy adult has around 35 trillion red blood cells, which make up about 40-45% of blood's volume.

"White blood cells, also called leukocytes, help fight infections and support the immune system. There are five types of white blood cells.

"Platelets, also called thrombocytes, help prevent and stop bleeding."

After that, Mrs. Crudlen curled her fingers into a fist and flexed her wrinkled-looking arm, and the muscles in her upper arm bulged out like weightlifters. Then, she began talking about muscle cells.

"Muscle cells form muscle tissue, enabling all bodily movement and helps maintain body temperature.

"The three types of muscle cells are skeletal, cardiac, and smooth. Skeletal muscle cells are attached to bones and are responsible for voluntary movements such as walking and running. Cardiac muscle cells are found in the heart and are responsible for pumping blood throughout the body. They contract and relax to make your heartbeat. They are involuntarily and move on their own. Smooth muscle cells also move on their own. They help with digestion, blood flow regulation, and bladder function."

Mrs. Crudlen grinned and exclaimed, "Here are some more! Digestive cells are specialized cells lining the digestive tract, responsible for breaking down and absorbing nutrients from food.

"Bone cells regulate the balance between bone formation and breakdown, known as bone remodeling. They also help mineralize bone tissue by producing and secreting minerals like calcium and phosphorus.

"Nerve cells, or neurons, transmit electrical and chemical signals throughout the body to enable communication. There are approximately 100 billion nerve cells in the body. Most of them are in the brain. They consist of three main parts: dendrites, axons, and synapses. Dendrites are branched extensions at the cell body that receive signals from other neurons. The axon is a long fiber that carries impulses away from the cell body to communicate with other neurons or muscles. The synapse is the junction between two neurons where neurotransmitters are released to transmit signals from one neuron to another. They have been described as looking like a star with a tail or a tree with branches and roots. Together, these three components enable the communication and coordination of the nervous system.

"Stem cells are found throughout the body, mainly the bone marrow. They can potentially develop into various cell types in the body and regenerate damaged tissue.

"Skin cells form the skin's protective outer layer and maintain its health and integrity.

"Fat cells store energy in the form of fat and regulate metabolism, which changes food into energy."

Mrs. Crudlen stopped talking, and her lips turned slightly upward at the corners. A glint of confidence in her eyes hinted at her knowledge of cells.

Then, with a gentle, modest smile, and sincerity in my voice, I said, "That was great information, but you didn't say anything about how cells reproduce, age, and when and how they die."

Mrs. Crudlen glared at me for a brief second. Then she began to speak, her voice strong, sounding like a professional actor on stage.

"Ah, life… it is a symphony. Every beat of our hearts, every breath we take, is a note in this grand composition. And the players, well… they are our cells—trillions of them, each with its own role, its own part in the music."

She paused; her eyes bright with wonder. "Let me tell you about these miraculous performers. You see, life begins with what I like to call a dance. Human cells reproduce through a process called cell division, where a single cell splits into two identical daughter cells. The process involves a series of tightly regulated steps. Cell division can be broadly categorized into two main types: mitosis and meiosis. Mitosis is the process by which body cells divide and create copies of themselves for growth and repair. In meiosis, the new cells have half the parent cell's genetic material, which is the process by which egg and sperm cells are formed to have a baby."

Her tone became more reflective and somber, yet still respectful. "But time, you see, time has its toll. Our cells—they grow old, just as I have. They begin to show signs of wear and tear, their membranes become less flexible, their ability to communicate with other cells diminishes, and their energy production falters. It is a natural part of life. Aging also happens when tiny errors sometimes creep into the DNA or the cell's components wear out from use.

Mrs. Crudlen paused. "Eventually, cells die. Cells can die in a couple of ways, which can be part of a natural process or due to injury. Apoptosis—the gentle goodbye. It is a programmed cell death, a planned exit, graceful like a bow after the final note of a musical. Apoptosis occurs when a cell is no longer needed or is damaged beyond repair. The cell receives signals to self-destruct. It breaks down its components and is cleaned up by other cells. This process is very orderly and helps keep the body healthy by removing cells that could potentially become harmful. When the cells on the surface of our bodies die, they are sloughed off and discarded and some come off when we wash them off. Those inside of our bodies, like in the lining of our gut, are scavenged by phagocytes where white blood cells ingest other cells, and the energy from the dead cells is partly recycled to make other white cells. However, if there is an injury and a cell is damaged by external factors like injury, infection, toxins, or failure of blood supply, necrosis occurs. Necrosis is the death of most or all the cells where they swell and burst, spilling their contents into the surrounding area. This can cause inflammation and damage to nearby cells."

She leaned toward me, her eyes blazing with intensity. "Yet even with all this—do you know how resilient we are? How life carries on? Cells can live from a few days to a year, or more. The cells in our bodies are replaced every 7 to 10 years. Some cells are exceptionally durable, and some are not. Cells in your digestive tract live for a few days, while cells in your immune system live up to six weeks. Cells in the brain have a longer lifespan than you do.

"Every single day, your body creates over 330 billion new cells. And just as many die—each one playing its part, giving way for the next. It is a ceaseless, magnificent cycle. Creation, renewal, aging, and death are woven into this vast symphony of life."

She leaned back in her rocking chair, her face serene, her eyes twinkling. "So here I am, at age 90. I may have fewer notes left in me, but I will tell you this—the music is still alive. The dance and music of mitosis, the quiet dignity of apoptosis are all there, still playing their parts."

She closed her eyes as if savoring the sound of an invisible melody. "Life… such a fragile, powerful, and wondrous thing. Cherish it while you have it."

When Mrs. Crudlen stopped talking, I watched closely as she inhaled and filled her lungs. When she exhaled, I could almost feel a release of tension leave me from my comments about her omitting something. However, I soon discovered that was my imagination.

"Mimi, I planned on talking about cell reproduction, aging, and cell death." Her brows furrowed deeply. "So, if you do not mind, I would like us to resume our conversation tomorrow. And if you do not mind, I would appreciate you discussing the types of tissues in the body tomorrow before we talk about organs and the eleven body systems." She paused with raised eyebrows and a confident smile. Then, she held her head up straight and slightly tilted it downward in a quick and deliberate motion and said, "Is that okay with you?"

"Yes, ma'am. I'd be glad to talk about body tissues," I replied, wishing I had kept my mouth shut about cell reproduction, aging, and death.

CHAPTER 5

Tissues

$\mathbf{M}$rs. Crudlen and I sat in our designated rocking chairs the following day. She had my undivided attention, and the conversation immediately went to the miraculous tissues in our bodies. I was glad I did my homework last night on the internet and that there were only four types of tissues in the body that I needed to remember and discuss. Hoping to give a powerful presentation, I straightened my posture and focused my eyes on Mrs. Crudlen. After a subtle smile that I hoped radiated a sense of confidence in myself, the words about body tissues quickly flowed from my mouth.

"There are four main types of tissues in the body. Epithelial, connective, muscle, and nervous tissue. Each tissue type serves a specific function, supporting the body's structure and functions.

"Epithelial tissue contains closely packed cells, single or multiple layers. It is a protective layer of cells that covers the surfaces of the body. It is located on the outermost layer of the skin and lines the cavities and organs within the body, such as the respiratory tract and digestive system. Epithelial tissue serves several vital functions, including acting as a barrier to protect against pathogens and harmful substances, regulating the exchange of molecules and ions, helping in the secretion of hormones, enzymes, nutrients, and other vital substances, and providing sensory information, such as touch.

"Connective tissue is a type of tissue found throughout the body that connects different tissues and organs to one another. They provide support and structure. Connective tissue is the most diverse and abundant class of tissues in various body parts, including tendons, ligaments, bones, cartilage, fatty tissue, collagen, lymph, and blood. Lymph and blood connect systems in the body, so they are called connective tissues. The structure of connective tissue varies depending on its location and function, with features like elasticity, flexibility, and strength. Its functions include connecting, cushioning, and protecting organs, storing energy, and aiding the immune response.

"Muscle tissue is found throughout the body and plays a critical role in movement, support, and heat production. It is divided into three main types: skeletal muscle tissue, cardiac muscle tissue, and smooth muscle tissue. Skeletal muscle is attached to bones with tendons and is responsible for voluntary movements such as walking and lifting. You have control over these muscles. The cardiac muscle is found in the heart and pumps blood throughout the body. It is involuntary; you have no control over it. Smooth muscle is in the walls of internal organs and blood vessels. It controls involuntary movements like peristalsis in the gut and helps regulate blood flow. You have no control over it.

"Nervous tissue is in the brain, spinal cord, and wherever nerves are located throughout the body. Its primary role is to transmit and integrate signals, allowing communication between different body parts and coordinating various bodily functions. In the brain, it is responsible for processing information, controlling movements, and regulating bodily functions. In the spinal cord, it acts as a pathway for signals traveling to and from the brain. Nervous tissue extends throughout the body, connecting organs and tissues to the central nervous system.

"Together, these tissues work harmoniously to maintain the body's overall health and function!"

When I finished my presentation, I was proud of it, but I noticed I talked with a monotone pitch and deliberate pronunciation of each word, like an automated sound. Apparently, Mrs. Crudlen noticed it, too.

"Mimi Mathis, you sounded like a robot! Did you use Artificial Intelligence to get information about tissues in our bodies?"

"Yes ma'am. I like AI."

"I do, too," she quickly replied. "That is fine that you used it. While AI can help us achieve our goals and improve efficiency, productivity, and convenience, there are also risks associated with its widespread use. For instance, job displacement, privacy concerns, errors, ethical dilemmas, and the potential for AI to be used maliciously, like causing older women to talk like robots. It is crucial to approach the integration of AI into our world thoughtfully and ethically to ensure that we reap the benefits of this technology while preventing its potential negative impacts. And I declare that AI will not control humans or replace human intelligence, and AI is not caring and compassionate! We must ensure we use it sensibly and ethically as you did." She paused, then said, "I prefer DI to AI any day."

"What is DI?" I asked, without sounding like a robot.

"DI is Divine Intelligence." She smiled. "Now, let us just use our intelligence and move on. Are you ready?"

"Yes, I am!"

"Good," she replied enthusiastically, making me want to hear more. "We will start with organs. An individual organ is made of the same type of well-organized tissue that works together to perform special functions. Each organ does a special job for your body. Your heart, lungs, brain, and stomach are organs. There are seventy-eight organs in your body. Five of them are needed for you to survive. If your heart, liver, brain, kidneys, and lungs stopped working and you did not have medical intervention, you would die. I will discuss organs more when I talk about the eleven Body Systems where organs and tissues come together to form systems."

She paused and smiled a smile that lit up her eyes. "Mimi, there is much more about basic Anatomy and Physiology for us to discuss. I like sharing information; it is like a gentle tug at the feel-good strings of my heart, wanting me to do more. Thank you for asking me to help you with your book."

"I thank you! I had forgotten how remarkable our bodies are. It makes me appreciate my old body more than ever," I replied.

"Good! I will ride that wave of euphoria of thankfulness with you before I delve into the body systems, starting with the M in Mrs. Crudlen & I."

We sat still, and in our moment of silence, every breath I took felt like a gift, and every heartbeat was a reminder of the abundance of life in my body.

Mrs. Crudlen looked at me and said, "The human body is amazing!"

CHAPTER 6
The Muscular System

Mrs. Crudlen and I faced each other, sitting in straight-back chairs across the small, sturdy oak table. With her silver hair tied back in a neat bun, she flexed her fingers, brows furrowed, and clenched her fist, revealing a sense of defiance and determination. I grinned back at her, my gray, curly hair looking wild and unruly. Writing this book with her had its challenging moments. Today, however, was a different kind of challenge—an arm-wrestling contest!

"Ready, Mimi?" Mrs. Crudlen asked, her eyes twinkling with mischief.

"As I'll ever be," I replied, my voice steady and determined.

We clasped hands, each feeling strength and warmth in the other's grip.

"Three, two, one, go!" I shouted, and the contest began.

At first, our hands stayed locked, muscles taut, and faces set in concentration. Gradually, however, Mrs. Crudlen began to gain the upper hand. My arm trembled as I struggled to push back, but Mrs. Crudlen's strength was undeniable.

"Do you know what's happening right now, Mimi?" Mrs. Crudlen asked, her voice calm and steady as her muscles bulged and veins stood out against her skin. "It's quite miraculous."

I grunted in response, my eyes fixed on our clasped hands.

"You see," Mrs. Crudlen continued, "when I decide to move my arm, which is a voluntary act of my skeletal muscles, it all starts in my brain."

My arm wavered, but Mrs. Crudlen held steady, her voice a soothing counterpoint to the physical struggle as she continued, "My brain sends a signal through my spinal cord and then to my arm muscles through motor neurons. These motor neurons then transmit the signals through the nervous system to the muscle fibers. A chemical reaction occurs once the signal reaches the muscle fibers, and loads of tiny muscle cells work together to make the muscle shorter. This shortening causes the muscle to contract, creating a pulling force—this contraction or pulling force results in the movement of the attached bones. Muscles work in pairs, with one muscle contracting while the other relaxes to allow for movement in opposite directions. This coordinated team effort enables us to perform a wide range of actions."

Sweat beaded on my forehead, but I couldn't help but be captivated by Mrs. Crudlen's description, even as I fought to stay in the game.

"Our muscles also need energy to keep contracting," she said, her breath coming a bit faster now. "This energy comes from ATP produced by the mighty mitochondria. They produce ATP through cellular respiration, using oxygen and nutrients from our food. That is why staying active and eating well is important."

With a final push, Mrs. Crudlen brought my hand down to the table! Then she released my hand and gave me a warm smile. "You did not put up much of a fight, Mimi. You do not have much muscle strength."

I ignored her last remark and shook my head in amazement. "That was a great review about muscle physiology," I said, rubbing my arm-wrestling arm.

"Good. Now, relax as I talk more about the magnificent muscular system."

"I'm ready," I replied, rubbing my sore hand.

"The muscular system is truly fascinating! Did you know that some experts say there are over 800 muscles in the human body? The marvelous muscular system is composed of muscles that work together with the skeletal system to create movement and help maintain body temperature. The main functions include movement, stability, structural support, and the source of nutrients such as amino acids, posture, heat production, and energy production during starvation. Now, I'm going to talk about some specific terms.

"Fascia is not a muscle, but a connective tissue that surrounds and supports the body's muscles, organs, and other structures. I am talking about it because it plays a role in facilitating movement by allowing muscles to glide smoothly over one another, which prevents friction. Additionally, fascia contains nerves and blood vessels, especially in the deep parts of the body.

"Muscles are located throughout the body and are attached to bones via tendons. They are classified into three main types. They are the same names as the three muscle tissues we discussed earlier. The skeletal muscles are responsible for voluntary movements, meaning you have control over these muscles. The smooth muscles move independently and control involuntary movements in internal organs and blood vessels. You have billions of smooth muscle cells. The cardiac muscles are found in the heart and are responsible for pumping blood. Cardiac muscles contract involuntarily and are the most used muscles in the body as they constantly keep pumping blood throughout your life. Muscles use glucose for energy. Proper nutrition, hydration, and regular exercise are essential for maintaining healthy and strong muscles.

"Your skeletal muscles make up 40% to 50% of your body weight. After age 40, or even 30, your skeletal muscle mass begins to decline. However, exercise can increase the size and strength of muscles. The largest muscle in your body is the outermost muscle in the buttock, the gluteus maximus or glutes. Your strongest muscle is your masseter for chewing food on each side of your jaw. It lifts the lower jaw mandible to close your mouth. The muscles of your eyes are the most active muscles. Your tongue is a set of eight muscles. It is the only muscle in your body that can actively contract and extend and is not connected to bone at both ends. Your tongue allows you to speak, chew, suck, or swallow in a coordinated way and has up to 4,000 taste buds.

"Muscles need oxygen, so the circulatory system brings oxygen and nutrients to the muscles. Lactic acid provides a backup energy source in the muscular system when oxygen levels are low. While lactic acid can cause muscle fatigue and soreness, it can also be used by the body as fuel for energy production, buff muscle acidity, and usually is not dangerous.

"Other systems are connected to the muscular system. They are the digestive, respiratory, and immune systems. It is just another testament that no two systems are independent.

"Tendons and ligaments are essential to the human body's musculoskeletal system. Tendons are tough, flexible cords of tissue that connect muscles to bones, allowing for movement and stability. Ligaments are strong bands of fibrous tissue that connect bones to bones, providing support and stability to joints. Together, tendons and ligaments work in harmony to facilitate smooth and coordinated movement, protect joints from excessive stress, and maintain the overall structural integrity of the body."

Mrs. Crudlen stood, walked in front of me, and stopped. "When I point to a place on my body, tell me the name of the muscle, and I'll tell you what it does."

"Okay. Let's do it!"

She quickly bent her right forearm and pointed to her right upper arm with her left pointer finger.

I immediately said, "Biceps."

"Yes. Biceps are responsible for elbow flexion, help control the shoulder and elbow joints, and move the arms forward, sideways, and upwards at the shoulder."

Next, she moved her finger to the back of the bicep.

"Triceps!" I exclaimed.

"Yes. The triceps extend the elbow, allowing you to straighten your arm." She glanced at my triceps and added, "It is also called a flabby arm in some older people."

Then, she quickly pointed to the outside of the upper arm, on top of the shoulder joint, where the upper arm meets the body's trunk.

"Deltoid," I said.

"Yes. The deltoid is a large triangular muscle found in the shoulder. It allows for movement of the arm around the shoulder joint."

Next, she pointed to the back of her neck and said, "This muscle stretches from the neck to the middle of the back."

"Trapezius!"

"Yes. The trapezius assists in shoulder movement, posture, tilting your head and neck, and twisting your arm."

She pointed to the front of the thigh, moving her right pointer finger fast with precision and agility.

"Quadriceps!"

"Yes. The quadriceps help extend your knees, keep the kneecap in place, and carry body weight. We call them quads at the gym where I go."

Next, she patted her leg behind her quadriceps.

"Hamstrings!"

"Yes. They assist in knee flexion and are essential for walking, running, jumping, and squatting. They flex the knee and extend the hip joint. The hamstrings work together with the quadriceps to provide stability and movement in the lower body."

She moved her finger up and pointed to her buttocks.

"The gluteal muscles, often called glutes."

"Correct. They are a group of three muscles that make up the gluteal region commonly known as the buttocks: the gluteus maximus, gluteus medius, and gluteus minimus. The three muscles originate from the pelvis and insert on the thigh bone."

After that, she pointed to the back of her lower leg.

"Gastrocnemius," I proudly announced.

"Good. The gastrocnemius muscles are a pair of muscles in the lower back leg, forming the bulk of the calf. They are known for their diamond shape and are often called the calf muscles. The gastrocnemius muscles are connected to the heel bone, calcaneus, by the Achilles tendon, one of the strongest tendons in the human body. This tendon allows the muscles to flex the foot at the ankle joint, enabling movements such as pointing the toes downward. Additionally, the gastrocnemius muscles are supported by various ligaments in the ankle and foot, providing stability and strength during physical activities like running, jumping, and walking."

Then Mrs. Crudlen held up both hands with ease and speed, wiggled her fingers, and said, "Fingers do not have muscles, but muscles in the hands attached to tendons in the fingers make fingers move. Each hand has 34 muscles. Hand movements are mostly started by movement of muscles in the forearm...you do not need to name them."

Next, she pointed to her abdomen.

"Abdominals or abs or Rectus Abdominis."

"Correct. The abs in the abdomen help trunk flexion, support the stomach, organs, bones, and spine, and help with core balance and stability. The core includes the muscles between your hips and the trapezius."

Mrs. Crudlen stopped talking. Her eyes widened with a subtle furrow of the eyebrows, conveying a look of curiosity. I immediately thought that whatever she was thinking was about me. And I must admit that dealing with her remarks has been challenging. But if she makes a strange remark about me this time, I'll lessen the impact by not taking it personally. I'll focus on the positive interactions with her and not give the remarks too much power over my emotions. I sat up straight, put on my imaginary suit of armor, and felt prepared for any critical comments.

"Mimi, when approaching the sensitive topic of someone's health, it is important to express genuine concern and care. That is why I want you to know that my intention and words about you are to support and offer help, not to be critical. Mimi, I care about you and noticed that your muscles have atrophied. Would you like me to talk about muscle atrophy and what can be done about it?"

I looked into her eyes and saw a caring look, like a gentle, soft, warm embrace. I felt a slight twinge of guilt for prejudging her before she talked, so I nodded yes.

"Muscle atrophy is a physical process that occurs when muscle tissue wastes away or decreases in size. It can be partial or complete, resulting in a loss of muscle function. Muscle atrophy, called sarcopenia, can begin as early as when a person turns 30 or 40 as part of the natural aging process. This process can continue at a loss of muscle mass at 1–8% per decade, depending on the person's activity level and other factors. Some may lose as much as 8% of their muscle mass each decade. Muscle loss can accelerate after age 65 and 75 and be more noticeable in lower body muscles. This causes a person to lose strength. Losing strength can increase the risk of falls and injuries.

"Muscle atrophy can be caused by disuse when people have an inactive lifestyle and stop doing activities that use muscle power. Muscles can weaken or atrophy when nerve cells cannot signal to the muscles, which is a neurogenic disease. Muscle atrophy can also be caused by diseases such as obesity, cancer, diabetes, renal failure, malnutrition, spinal cord or peripheral nerve injuries, stroke, or long-term corticosteroid therapy, as well as severe burns and starvation. Athletes can start losing muscle after just three weeks of inactivity.

Muscle atrophy can also occur when someone becomes bedridden or after an injury.

"However, the good news is that activity and strength training can help people maintain and rebuild muscle at any age. Regular exercise, especially resistance training exercises that help build and maintain muscle strength, is important to prevent muscle loss. Also, consuming enough protein in the diet, staying hydrated, getting enough quality sleep, and managing stress can all contribute to preventing muscle loss."

Though gentle in delivery, her message held a powerful weight that impacted me. It was as if her knowledge enriched the sound of her voice, adding depth to every syllable, and was meant to help me.

"Thank you so much! I needed to hear that," I said with sincere gratitude.

"Good. Now get off your gluteus maximus, gluteus medius and gluteus minimus, and go walking! Make sure it is brisk and not slow!"

CHAPTER 7

The Respiratory System

"Mimi, let us talk about the miraculous and impressive respiratory system."

"Ok. Sounds breathtaking," I said, then snickered.

Mrs. Crudlen gave me a thumbs up and said, "The respiratory system is an intricate network of organs and tissues that takes oxygen from the air you breathe in, called inhalation, and delivers it to the blood. When you breathe out, called exhalation, it sends carbon dioxide out of the body. The system consists of the nose, pharynx, larynx, trachea, bronchi, lungs, ribs, intercostal muscles, and diaphragm."

When Mrs. Crudlen stopped talking, I automatically inhaled deeply, filling my lungs with life-giving fresh air. Next, I held my breath for seven seconds. Then, slowly and steadily, I released my breath, feeling tension leave with it.

"Mimi Mathis, your deep breathing was a simple yet powerful act of self-care. Now, I would like to talk more about the organs in the respiratory system." She smiled, took a deep breath, and let it out.

"The respiratory system is like a beautiful set of pipes and bellows in an old church organ, each part working together to keep your breath flowing smoothly."

"Where does it all start?" I asked.

Mrs. Crudlen pointed to the back of her head. "The part of the brain that controls breathing is called the medulla oblongata, located at the very bottom of the brain where it connects to the spinal cord. The medulla constantly monitors carbon dioxide levels in the blood and sends signals to the muscles involved in breathing to adjust accordingly." Then she pointed to her nose and said, "The air first enters through the nose. Your nostrils are holes that lead to your nasal cavities. The nasal septum is a wall of cartilage and thin bone that separates the nasal passages and divides the nose into two nasal cavities. The front part of the septum is made of cartilage and covered by skin with many blood vessels, while the back part is made of bone. Did you ever have a bloody nose? The septum is covered on both sides by a mucous membrane. The cute little hairs and mucus in your nose trap dirt and dust that would otherwise end up in your nasal passages.

"Inside, along the sides of both nasal cavities, are bony structures called nasal conchae. They help increase the surface area inside the nasal cavity, which aids in warming, humidifying, and filtering the air we breathe. The nasal sinuses are four paired air-filled cavities within the facial bones connected to the nasal cavity. They are behind the forehead, nasal bones, cheeks, and eyes. They lighten the skull and enhance our voice resonance. The nasal sinuses are lined with a mucous membrane that produces mucus to moisten the nasal passages and trap dust and other particles, helping to humidify and filter the air we breathe. Mucus is a slimy, slippery substance, sometimes called snot, boogers, gunk, or phlegm. I have been called snotty when I have called others little boogers. Most of the time, mucus drains out, and air flows easily through the sinuses. When the nasal sinuses become inflamed or infected, it can cause congestion, facial pain, and headaches."

"And those hurts!" I exclaimed.

"Exactly! And when you are in a rush or need more air, you can breathe through your mouth.

"The nasal cavity also contains olfactory receptors responsible for our sense of smell. The nose has 400 receptors to pick up odors and send signals along nerves to the brain. They can distinguish between numerous smells and have a direct line of emotion and memory to the brain. For example, the tongue's taste buds identify taste, and the nerves in the nose identify smell. Both sensations are communicated to the brain, integrating the information to recognize and appreciate flavors."

Mrs. Crudlen raised her forefinger and traced an imaginary line down her throat.

"After the nose, air goes into the pharynx, also known as the throat. It is a muscular tube behind the nasal cavity, mouth, and voice box. The average adult size is about 5 inches long. It is a shared space for both air and food. During breathing, the pharynx filters, warms, and humidifies incoming air before it reaches the lungs. It also houses the tonsils, immune system components that help fight off respiratory infections.

"Then, the air heads to the larynx—your voice box, where your vocal cords live. The larynx vibrates when air passes through, producing sound for speech. Muscles within the larynx control the tension and position of the vocal cords, allowing for adjustments in pitch and volume of the voice. It also plays a crucial role in swallowing by closing off the airway to prevent food and liquids from entering the lungs. The epiglottis is a flap of tissue at the base of the tongue that covers the larynx during swallowing to direct food and liquid into the esophagus and away from the airway. This clever, life-saving spoon-shaped elastic epiglottis cartilage prevents food and liquids from going down the wrong way. Good for the epiglottis!"

Mrs. Crudlen continued, "From the larynx, the air moves down the trachea—your windpipe. It is a sturdy tube with cartilage rings, like a vacuum hose, so it stays open and does not collapse. The trachea splits into two big branches called bronchi—one for each lung. The right main bronchus is shorter, more comprehensive, and more vertical than the left one, which is narrower and more horizontal. The bronchi are lined with cilia and mucus-producing cells that help trap and remove particles and microorganisms from the air we breathe into our lungs. The bronchi keep branching into smaller tubes called bronchioles until they reach tiny air sacs called alveoli located in the lungs.

"The lungs are two vital organs located in the chest cavity, called the thorax. The lungs exchange oxygen and carbon dioxide within the blood. Each lung is divided into lobes. The right lung has three lobes, while the left has two to accommodate the heart. The lungs are also protected by the rib cage and pleura, a smooth double-layered membrane with a space in between called the pleural cavity. This space has fluid in it to keep everything gliding smoothly while you breathe.

"Within the lungs are around 300 to 500 million tiny air sacs called alveoli where gas exchange occurs. Each alveolus looks like a grape-like structure and is surrounded by a network of blood vessels called capillaries, where oxygen from the inhaled air diffuses into the bloodstream. In contrast, carbon dioxide diffuses out of the blood and into the alveoli to be exhaled."

"That's where the magic happens!"

"Not exactly," she replied. "Magic happens all through the parts we discussed and in a dome-shaped muscle that sits under the lungs. It is called the diaphragm. When you breathe in, the diaphragm flattens out, giving your lungs more room to expand. Then, when you breathe out, it pops back up, pushing the air out. Neck and intercostal muscles between the ribs help move the rib cage, which assists breathing."

"I sighed contentedly. "I agree; it is all like magic, one breath at a time."

"Speaking of breathing—deep breathing, called diaphragmatic or abdominal breathing, is a simple yet powerful practice that can benefit our bodies and minds. When we take deep breaths, we bring more oxygen into our lungs, which helps to improve our overall lung capacity and efficiency. This can lead to more energy, improved focus and concentration, and even a boost in our immune system. Deep breathing also helps to reduce stress and anxiety by activating the body's relaxation response. By slowing down our breath, we signal to our nervous system that it is safe to relax, which can help to lower our heart rate and blood pressure. This can have a calming effect on our mind and body, promoting feelings of peace and well-being.

"Before I finish, I want to tell you a few fascinating respiratory system features. Forty-three facial, head, and neck muscles are involved in breathing and speaking. A strong sneeze can travel up to 100 miles per hour. It helps clear out irritants from the respiratory system. The average adult takes about 12-20 breaths per minute, around 17,000-30,000 breaths daily. That is around 500 milliliters of air. 1 tsp = 4.929 milliliters. You do the math, Mimi!"

After taking a few deep breaths, Mrs. Crudlen looked at me and said, "Everyone's breath is as important to them as your breath is to you, and mine is to me. We must never forget that."

CHAPTER 8

The Skeletal System

"It is time to talk about the miraculous skeletal system. First, I will walk for you, then I will describe what happens to the skeletal system when I walk. So, Mimi, please watch me. Watch me. Watch me walk like Marilyn Monroe." Mrs. Crudlen quickly stood, and I gasped in amazement as she walked across the lawn and back.

Mrs. Crudlen's walk was captivating and effortless, exuding confidence and grace with each step she took, one foot in front of the other. She possessed a unique blend of sensuality and elegance in her gait, with subtle hip movements that moved from side to side. She had a slight bounce in her step, adding a playful quality to her walk. Her arms swung gracefully at her side and her stride was smooth and fluid, gliding across the lawn as if floating on air. When she sat back down in her rocking chair, she said, "Walking is the basic human locomotion where we move by alternating our legs in a coordinated manner to propel our body forward." Her voice was soft and breathy, with a slightly playful tone.

"You walked like Marilyn Monroe, and you sounded like her!" I cried out.

"I know it," she replied, winked at me, and resumed talking in her usual tone.

"Walking is a fundamental human movement that involves the coordination of various body systems to propel the body forward in a rhythmic manner. Our bones cannot move on their own. The brain initiates and regulates movement, then muscles move the bones by pulling them. The skeletal system provides the framework for movement, the muscles contract and relax to create motion, and the joints allow for flexibility and stability. Walking requires the cardiovascular system to deliver oxygen and nutrients to the muscles, the respiratory system to provide oxygen for energy production, and the nervous system to control muscle contractions and balance. This intricate process enables humans to walk smoothly and efficiently, demonstrating the remarkable coordination between various systems in the body."

"It is remarkable that our body works together like that!" I replied.

"I know it. I am ready to give you a good overview of the skeletal system," she quickly responded.

"The skeletal system comprises bones, cartilage, tendons, ligaments, and joints. These structures work together to provide support, protection, and movement. The bones serve as the framework of the body. Your muscles provide the energy to move! Bones support muscles and organs while also protecting vital organs like the brain and heart. Bones store minerals like calcium, magnesium, and phosphorus, and they produce blood cells in the bone marrow.

"The skeletal system consists of 206 bones, each with a specific shape and function. Out of 206 bones, 172 of them are pairs. Bones make up about 15% of your total body weight.

"Bones in the human body are divided into several categories based on their location and function. The cranial bones form the skull and protect the brain. These include the frontal, parietal, occipital, temporal, sphenoid, and ethmoid bones. The ribcage is formed by the sternum, called the breastbone, the thoracic vertebra, and 12 pairs of ribs. These protect the heart and lungs. The shoulder blade, the scapula, is a flat, triangular bone on the upper back that connects to the clavicle or collarbone. The clavicle runs horizontally across the front of the shoulder and acts like a rod to support the arm. Together, the scapula and clavicle form the bony framework of the shoulder joint, providing stability and mobility for arm movements. The spinal column, or vertebral column, is made up of 33 vertebrae that protect the spinal cord and support the body. The pelvis consists of the hip bones, ilium, ischium, and pubis, which support the body's weight and protect the reproductive organs. The upper extremities include the humerus, radius, ulna, carpals, metacarpals, and phalanges, which make up the arms and hands. The lower extremities consist of the femur, patella, tibia, fibula, tarsals, metatarsals, and phalanges, which comprise the legs and feet. The smallest bone in the human body is the stapes in the middle ear, while the longest bone is the femur in the thigh. Your skeleton renews itself entirely every ten years.

"Each bone consists of a hard outer layer called compact bone, which protects the inner spongy bone that contains bone marrow. Bone marrow is found in most bones and produces red blood cells, white blood cells, and platelets. Then, it sends them out into the blood to replace dead ones. There are two types of bone marrow: red marrow and yellow marrow. Red marrow is responsible for producing red blood cells, white blood cells, and platelets. It makes millions of blood cells daily. Yellow marrow primarily stores fat. Yellow marrow also serves as a reserve of nutrients and helps red marrow in case of a need for increased blood cell production demand, such as during illness or injury. Bones also contain blood vessels and nerves that supply them with nutrients and allow for sensation.

"Joints are the connections between bones that allow movement and flexibility. They come in distinct types. Hinge joints, such as the elbow and knee. The ball-and-socket joints in the hips and shoulders move in most directions. Saddle joints in the knuckles and wrist. Gliding joints in the ankles and wrist. And pivot joints, such as the top of the backbone, allow your head to turn from side to side.

"Synovial fluid, also known as joint fluid, is found in the cavities of movable joints. It reduces friction, cushions the ends of the bones, and provides nutrients.

"Ligaments allow joints to move while holding the bones together. They are bands of stretchy connective tissue that connect bones to each other, offering stability and support to the joints.

"Tendons are durable, fibrous tissues that link muscles to bones, acting like a string that ties muscles to bones.

"Cartilage is found in areas such as the joints, nose, ears, and between vertebrae in the spine. It grows at the end of bones and acts as a cushion between bones, absorbing shock and preventing friction during movement, allowing for smooth joint motion. It also helps maintain the shape of certain body parts. Although cartilage does not have its blood supply, it can repair and regenerate itself to some extent. However, due to its limited blood flow, cartilage injuries can take longer to heal compared to other tissues.

"I think that is a good overview of the skeletal system. Do you want to add anything about the skeletal system, Mimi?"

"Yes. Years ago, I wrote a song about bones. I used the tune to *Dry Bones* sung by the Delta Rhythm Boys." I cleared my throat, swallowed, and started singing,

"The body has 206 bones
Sing loud don't want to hear you groan.

We'll start at the top and go down until we stop
The facial bone connects to the skull's cranium
The cranium connects to the vertebrae

The cervical at the top number seven
Thoracic vertebrae number one plus eleven
The five below are called the lumbar
They are the strongest vertebrae by far
The 5 sacrum and 4 coccyx are the last two
They were little segments that fused as you grew
Now let's go up to the ribs

12 pairs of ribs attach to your spine in the back
The top 7 connect to your sternum in front
Lower 5 float around in front protecting your truck
The sternum connects to the
clavicle

The clavicle connects to the scapula
The scapula is also called the shoulder blade
Isn't it incredible how our bodies are made
So let's go down the arm

The humerus is connected to the ulna
The proximal end is called the olecranon
When you're sitting at the table it's used to lean on
On the thumb side is the radius.

The radius is connected to carpals. The carpals are
connected to metacarpals.

Metacarpals connected to the phalanges
A phalange is also called a finger
And you certainly are a good singer
So let's go down to the hip

The hip connects with the sacrum and the leg bone
I'd hate to make a living by writing songs
So let's sing about the pelvis
The pelvis is also known as your hip bones
The largest part is called the ilium
It connects in the back to the sacrum
The ilium connects to the ischium
The ischium connects to the pubis bone.
Now let's go down the leg

The biggest bone in our body is the femur
The femur is connected to the patella
If you don't know what that is I won't tell ya
So let's keep going down the leg
The patella is connected to the tibia
The tibia is connected to the fibula
Both are connected to the tarsals
Tarsals connect to the metatarsals
Metatarsals connect to the phalanges called toes
And that is as far as we go!"

Anxious to hear Mrs. Crudlen's opinion about my song, I burst out, "What do you think about my song?"

Mrs. Crudlen's response was like a reflex action—quick, instinctive, immediately revealing her opinion. And this is exactly what she said, "Mimi Mathis, just because it sounded stupid—don't mean it ain't!"

CHAPTER 9

The Circulatory System

"The Circulatory System, also called the Cardiovascular System, is a miraculous, complex network of blood vessels that transports oxygen, nutrients, and waste products throughout the body and helps regulate body temperature. The heart is the featured organ.

"The heart pumps about 1.5 gallons of blood every minute. An adult heart is about the size of two hands clasped together, while a child's heart is about the size of a fist. I have heard that the body has so many blood vessels that they could wrap around the world twice."

"Mrs. Crudlen, that was fun to hear," I replied. "Anything else fun?"

"Yes. I love to imagine and write, so I wrote a short story about a talking heart last night. And I would like to read it now."

"And I would love to hear it now," I replied.

"Lub-dub, lub-dub, lub-dub." That is me resonating with life. That lub-dub sound of a heartbeat is caused by the rhythmic closing of my heart valves as blood flows in and out of my chambers. Without me, you would have no life, no energy, no spark. I am responsible for pumping blood throughout the body, keeping every organ supplied with oxygen and nutrients.

Let me show you around. First, meet my chambers. I have four chambers. Two are on top, called the atria, and two are on the bottom, called the ventricles. Each chamber is separated by doors called valves that prevent blood backflow. The tricuspid valve separates the right atrium and ventricle. The mitral valve does the same on the left. The aortic and pulmonary valves act like security guards at the exit gates, ensuring blood flows smoothly in one direction.

Deoxygenated blood enters the right atrium, passing through the tricuspid valve, and into the right ventricle. From there, it is pumped through the pulmonary artery to the lungs for oxygenation. Oxygenated blood returns to me through the pulmonary veins, entering the left atrium, passing through the mitral valve, and into the left ventricle. The blood is then pumped out through the aorta to supply oxygen and nutrients to the body. Arteries carry oxygenated blood away from the heart, while veins return deoxygenated blood to the heart. I am a resilient muscular pump!

I work with precision, like a well-oiled machine, but I am more than just a pump. I have an electrical network that keeps everything in perfect sync. It all starts at the sinoatrial, SA node, often called the heart's natural pacemaker. The SA node sends out electrical signals that tell the atria to contract, pushing blood into the ventricles.

The signal then travels to the atrioventricular, AV node, which acts like a relay station, slowing down the signal just enough to let the ventricles fill. From there, the signal races down a network of special muscles called the Bundle of His and spreads through the Purkinje fibers that connect electrical signals to make the ventricles contract. I beat approximately 60-100 times per minute.

It is a beautiful dance, all in the name of keeping you alive. I pump about 2,000 gallons of blood through these vessels every day.

However, I do not work alone; I am lovingly wrapped in a protective double-layered sac called the pericardium. This cushion keeps me safe from friction as it pumps tirelessly. And I cannot do everything alone. I rely on my brain and a network of blood vessels—arteries, veins, and capillaries—to carry out my mission.

My brain controls me; we are remarkably close, even inseparable. The brain controls me through a complex network of signals and nerves. This exciting process is mainly governed by the autonomic nervous system, which consists of two main branches: the sympathetic and parasympathetic nervous systems. When the brain senses a need for me to beat faster, such as during exercise or in response to stress, it sends signals through the sympathetic nervous system to increase the heart rate. On the other hand, when the body needs to relax or during rest, the parasympathetic nervous system sends signals to slow down the heart rate.

Overall, the brain continuously monitors the body's needs and adjusts my heart rate accordingly to ensure that the body receives the right amount of blood and oxygen to function correctly. My primary purpose is to pump and circulate blood throughout the body. I work tirelessly to deliver oxygen and nutrients to every cell in the body, while also removing waste products and carbon dioxide. I help maintain the body's overall function and balance. I am essentially a powerhouse that keeps you alive.

The End

"Mrs. Crudlen, that was an informative and delightful story about the heart," I responded.

"Thank you. I am glad you like it. Now, I will talk about blood vessels.

"The circulatory system, a marvel of nature, is linked together in one big system with a complex network of blood vessels, each playing a vital role in our survival. This network includes arteries, veins, and capillaries. They carry blood to every cell in your body from head to toe. They work in harmony to ensure proper circulation of blood throughout the body. They deliver essential nutrients and oxygen while removing waste products.

"Blood vessels leading out of the heart are called arteries. Arteries carry oxygen-rich blood from the heart to various body parts. They deliver nutrients and oxygen to the tissues and organs. They have thick, muscular walls that allow them to withstand the high pressure exerted by the pumping action of the heart. The largest artery in the body is the aorta, which originates from the left ventricle of the heart and branches out into smaller arteries throughout the body.

"Blood vessels leading back to the heart are called veins. Veins carry oxygen-depleted blood back to the heart. They have thinner walls compared to arteries, as they operate under lower pressure. Veins are equipped with valves that prevent blood from flowing backward, ensuring it moves toward the heart efficiently. These vessels are responsible for transporting waste products and carbon dioxide from the body's tissues back to the heart and lungs for oxygen.

"Capillaries are the smallest and most numerous blood vessels in the body. They connect arteries and veins. These tiny blood vessels have thin walls, allowing oxygen and nutrients from the blood to move through the walls to the cells and remove their waste products. They are essential for ensuring vital molecules reach their destinations.

"Beyond their role in circulation, the blood vessels also serve as an essential part of our body's temperature control system. When the body temperature rises, the blood vessels near the skin's surface dilate, called vasodilation, to release heat. Equally, when the body temperature drops, the blood vessels constrict to conserve heat.

"Blood in humans is a vital fluid that circulates in the body. There is a lot packed into one drop of blood. Blood has red blood cells, white blood cells, platelets, and plasma. Red blood cells are round, flat, and red. They contain hemoglobin, a protein that binds to oxygen and transports it everywhere in the body. White blood cells defend the body against infections and diseases. They are round and white with a bumpy surface. Platelets help with blood clotting to prevent excessive bleeding. They are small, round, and flat. They stretch out what looks like fingers to mend a wound. Plasma is the liquid component of about 55% of the total blood volume. It is a pale yellowish fluid made of about 92% water. It aids blood clotting and carries hormones, enzymes, proteins, and other substances."

I noticed Mrs. Crudlen's wrinkles deepen as her brows drew together and the corners of her mouth turned downwards, conveying a sense of unease.

"That was good information, but is something wrong?" I asked. "You look concerned."

"I am concerned. One person dies every 33 seconds in our country from cardiovascular disease. According to the American Heart Association three-fourths of people over seventy have some cardiovascular incident. The aging population needs to make certain to have check-ups by their healthcare provider for their heart health. Regular exercise like walking, or gardening, can do wonders for your heart. Trust me, no one will do it for them if they do not do it. When you care for your heart, you also care for your brain!"

"I promise that information will be in the book," I said.

Unexpectedly, Mrs. Crudlen placed her right hand over her heart and said, "This is my sign of respect for our majestic cardiovascular system, especially my heart. The saying 'has a big heart' is a common expression used to describe someone who is kind, compassionate, and caring toward others. When we say that someone has a big heart, we are acknowledging their capacity for empathy, generosity, selflessness, and genuine concern and compassion.

"I am as serious as a heartbeat when I say that the human heart is intricately connected to emotions, especially love. When we experience feelings of love, the brain releases hormones like oxytocin and dopamine, which trigger a range of emotional responses that are felt in the heart. This connection between the heart and love is not just metaphorical—studies have shown that emotions can directly impact heart health."

And the greatest is love!

CHAPTER 10

The Reproductive System

"R is for the reproductive system," Mrs. Crudlen announced. "It is a miraculous complex network of organs and glands that work together to facilitate the production of offspring, called having children. It also enables sexual function and produces hormones that support pregnancy and sexual development. It begins at puberty.

"Puberty is a natural process of physical and hormonal changes that occur as children transition into adolescence and adulthood. In females, puberty typically begins around the ages of 8-13 and involves the development of breasts, which are mammary glands made from connective tissue, fat, and tissue that contains glands that make milk. The growth of pubic hair and the start of menstruation is part of puberty. Hormonal changes in puberty lead to emotional and physical changes, such as mood swings and growth spurts. In males, puberty usually starts between the ages of 9-14. Obvious changes are the deepening of the voice, facial and body hair growth, and increased muscle mass. Hormonal changes also lead to the growth of the reproductive organs and the production of sperm in the male. Overall, puberty is a significant period of growth and development that prepares both females and males for adulthood and reproduction.

"The male reproductive system is used for urination and sexual relations. It is a network of internal and external organs primarily responsible for producing sperm, the male sex cells, and the hormone testosterone, which is crucial for male development and reproduction.

"Now, I will talk about the parts of the male reproductive system.

"Testes, or testicles, are two small, oval-shaped organs located in a pouch of skin outside the body called the scrotum. The scrotum helps regulate the temperature of the testes. They are the primary organs where sperm and testosterone are produced. Testosterone helps develop male traits and reproductive functions.

"Epididymis: A long, coiled tube behind and attached to each testicle is where sperm matures and becomes capable of movement.

"Vas deferens: A muscular tube that carries sperm from the epididymis to the to the urethra, where they are pushed out during ejaculation.

"Urethra: A tube that carries both urine and semen through the penis. Urine and semen are released from the body through the urethra at the tip of the penis.

"Ejaculation: During sexual arousal, sperm is released from the epididymis and mixed with fluids from the seminal vesicles that nourish sperm. This fluid, called semen, mixes with the sperm, which is then pushed through and out of the tip of the penis during ejaculation.

"Seminal Vesicles are glands located behind the bladder and produce a fluid that nourishes the sperm and helps them move more easily.

"Prostate gland: A gland located below the bladder and in front of the rectum surrounds the urethra and adds another fluid to semen. This helps protect and energize the sperm through the female reproductive system.

"Penis: The external male organ used for sexual intercourse and urination.

"The hypothalamus, a key player in the brain, not only triggers the pituitary gland to release hormones that encourage the testes to produce testosterone but also plays a significant role in sexual stimulation.

"To sum up, the male reproductive system works together to produce, store, and deliver sperm, allowing for the possibility of reproduction.

When a sperm meets an egg and fertilizes it, a zygote is created. The zygote goes through a process of becoming an embryo and developing into a fetus.

"Male reproduction is a continuous process of the production of sperm cells throughout a man's life. Unlike females who are born with a finite number of eggs, males can produce sperm cells from puberty onwards until old age. This means that males can technically reproduce their entire life, as long as they remain healthy and fertile. As men age, the quality of their sperm may decline, which can lead to a decrease in fertility and an increased risk of genetic mutations in offspring. Nonetheless, the potential for male reproduction persists throughout their lifespan."

Mrs. Crudlen paused, drank some water, and said, "The reproductive system is essential for the continuation of the species. Both males and females are needed to ensure successful reproduction. So now, let's talk about the female. And I will start with the ovaries.

"Ovaries are two small, almond-shaped organs on either side of the uterus. The hormones estrogen and progesterone from the ovaries control the reproductive system. They cause the body to release eggs, prepare the uterus for pregnancy, and trigger menstruation. Every month, one ovary releases an egg in a process called ovulation.

"Ovulation is a phase in the menstrual cycle when the ovary releases an egg called an ovum.

"Fallopian Tubes are thin tubes connecting the ovaries to the uterus. After ovulation, the egg travels down the fallopian tube. Fertilization typically occurs in the fallopian tube when a sperm meets the egg and then goes to the uterus.

"The uterus is a hollow, pear-shaped organ where a fetus develops during pregnancy. The uterus, or the womb, is between the bladder and rectum in the pelvis. If an egg is fertilized, it attaches to the uterus lining, and pregnancy begins. If the egg is not fertilized, the body sheds the uterus lining during menstruation, a monthly period.

"The cervix is an opening of the uterus that connects to the vagina. The cervix expands to allow a baby to pass through it when it is born. It is the normal passage during childbirth.

"The vagina is a muscular tube that extends from the cervix to the external private parts called genitalia. It is the passage through which menstrual blood leaves the body; it is used for sexual intercourse and the usual passage during childbirth.

"Vulva: The external female genitalia, including the labia majora, labia minora, clitoris, and vaginal opening.

"A menstrual cycle is a monthly process where a woman's body prepares for potential pregnancy by building up a uterine lining. If no pregnancy occurs, the uterine lining sheds as a menstrual period and starts the cycle over again. The menstrual fluid is blood, mucus, and other cellular debris from the uterus. This is controlled by hormones released from the ovaries. The body prepares for pregnancy each month until menopause.

"Menopause is the end of women's menstrual cycle and fertility, usually occurring in their late 40s to early 50s. During menopause, hormonal changes lead to symptoms like hot flashes, mood swings, and sleep disturbances. It is a natural biological process that signifies the end of a woman's reproductive years.

With grace, poise, and a steady voice, Mrs. Crudlen said, "The human reproductive system is awesome!" Then she smiled and said, with a sense of authority and powerful delivery, "The major function of the miraculous reproductive system is to ensure the survival of the species. The world population is 8.2 billion, so it appears to be working!"

CHAPTER 11

The Urinary System

"Well, Mimi, we have made it to the U in Mrs. Crudlen & I. The U stands for the Urinary System, also called the Renal System. Renal means kidney. The miraculous urinary system is a vital and incredible part of the human body. The urinary system is like a cleaning crew for your body. It helps get rid of waste and extra fluids by making urine. Think of it as a filtering system: it takes out the stuff you do not need from your blood, like toxins and extra water, and makes you urinate or pee, as younger generations call it. Your kidneys do most of the work by filtering your blood to produce urine, which then goes to your bladder to wait until you urinate. So, in simple terms, the urinary system helps keep your body clean and balanced by eliminating waste and extra fluids.

"It also does more. Are you ready to hear how it all works?"

I nodded, intrigued. "Yes!"

Mrs. Crudlen took a sip of her water and began, her voice steady and clear. "It all starts with our kidneys, those two bean-shaped organs sitting on either side of your spine, back of the abdominal cavity, just below your rib cage. They are small, around 1/3 pound, and about the size of a fist. But do not let their size fool you—they are powerful! Their main job is to filter our blood. They are like the body's natural detoxifiers. Every time your heart beats, it pumps blood into both of your kidneys. The kidneys filter about 52 gallons of blood a day, but only a small portion becomes urine."

Mrs. Crudlen leaned forward. "Kidneys can filter because of neurons. There are about a million nephrons, the little filtering units, in each kidney. Nephrons have different parts, but their glomerulus and the tubules do most of the work. Blood enters the glomerulus under high pressure. It is a network of tiny blood vessels where blood is filtered to remove waste and excess substances from the body. The tubules receive the filtered fluid from the glomerulus, reabsorb essential nutrients, and regulate water and electrolyte balance before the urine is formed. In simpler terms, the glomerulus is like a sieve that filters blood, while the tubules are like pipes that process the filtered substance to make urine.

"After reabsorption, what is left is urine, which is mostly waste products and extra water.

"Once urine is formed, it travels down from the kidneys to the bladder through the ureters, two thin tubes. The ureters, about 10 to 12 inches long, enter the bladder at an angle, forming a one-way valve that prevents urine from flowing back towards the kidneys. The ureters have muscles that contract rhythmically, pushing the urine down like squeezing toothpaste from a tube.

"Kidneys produce renin, a hormone which helps control blood pressure. Kidneys release erythropoietin, which tells your bone marrow to make more red blood cells when oxygen levels are low. They also make calcitriol, a hormone and active form of Vitamin D, responsible for regulating calcium levels in the blood, which is essential for strong bones and teeth."

I liked her explanation and was curious how she would explain the bladder. "And what about the bladder? It's just a storage space for urine, right?"

"Not just any storage space," she chuckled. "The bladder is remarkable. It is a stretchy, muscular sac in the pelvic region that holds urine until it is ready to release. The bladder has a capacity of approximately 400-600 milliliters, 400 milliliters is approximately two cups. People usually feel the need to urinate when their bladder has between 150 and 250 milliliters of urine in it. However, the amount can vary between individuals.

"When the bladder fills up, nerves in the bladder walls transmit signals to your brain, telling you it is time to empty it. The bladder is made of smooth muscle tissue, which contracts to expel urine from the body through the urethra during urination, also called peeing.

"The bladder has two sphincter muscles which allow urine to flow out. One you have no control over and one you control. During urination, the bladder muscles contract, and the sphincter muscles relax, allowing urine to flow through the urethra and out of the body. When the person is finished, the sphincter closes.

"In males, the urethra also plays a role in the reproductive system, serving as a pathway for both urine and semen. The male urethra passes through the prostate gland and penis before exiting the body. The female urethra opens in front of the vaginal opening. It is more susceptible to urinary tract infections."

I nodded thoughtfully. "The bladder is quite a delicate balance of muscles and nerves."

"Exactly," she said, her eyes twinkling with enthusiasm. "I have a few more important functions of the kidneys to talk about before we stop."

"What are they?" I asked.

"The kidneys regulate the body's fluid balance and electrolyte levels by controlling the amount of water, salts, and other things in our blood excreted in the urine. This balance is called homeostasis. When homeostasis is disrupted, as in dehydration, the kidneys adjust their function to help restore balance. For example, the kidneys can balance the body's acid-base balance by excreting hydrogen ions and reabsorbing bicarbonate from urine. Urine comprises approximately 95% water and 5% waste products and salts. The color of urine can vary depending on factors such as hydration levels, diet, and certain medical conditions."

Mrs. Crudlen leaned back and sighed. "It's amazing how much is happening inside us, even as we sit here sipping water." That said, we clinked our glasses together, savoring both the water and the words that flowed during our conversation.

Mrs. Crudlen picked up the water pitcher, filled our glasses, and raised her glass high. I did the same to show respect and celebrate whatever she was going to say. She looked me directly in my eyes, gently clinked our glasses, and said, "In honor of our urinary system we drink this water with gratitude. Cheers!"

"Cheers," I responded, then drank some more water.

Mrs. Crudlen glanced at me and asked, "Mimi, would you like to add anything about the urinary system before we stop talking about it?"

"No, ma'am, that was good. May I be excused?"

"Certainly, you may. It is the right door to your left when you go inside. In a healthy body, no matter how much water you take in, your kidneys ensure you have just the right amount."

CHAPTER 12

The Digestive System

"Mimi, six systems down and five to go! We have made it to the miraculous and delectable Digestive System, also called the Gastrointestinal System, or GI system. It is a wonderful network of organs working together to break down food into nutrients and energy so the body can use them for growth, repair, and tissue function. The digestive system also removes waste products that the body cannot use. In my eyes, this system is fascinating and almost magical." Mrs. Crudlen stopped talking and asked me to close my eyes. I did as she requested.

"Now, open your eyes, Mimi." I did and surprise, surprise! Mrs. Crudlen had on a shimmering pink gown adorned with delicate sparkles and twinkling sequins. She wore a crystal tiara that emitted a soft, enchanting light, and she held a wand with a sparkling gem at the tip. Her shoes were decorated with tiny pearls and crystals. She was dressed like a fairy godmother! And when she began talking, her voice sounded sweet and smooth.

"Once upon a time, there was a marvelous land known as the Gastrointestinal Realm. This enchanting land was home to many tissues and organs and other wondrous places, each playing a crucial role in transforming humble morsels into vital energy for the kingdom of a human.

"This tale begins in the Mouth, a vibrant and bustling village where the Teeth, Saliva, and Tongue live. The Teeth, solid and sturdy, chomped and crushed the food into tiny bits, preparing it for the next part of its journey. Immediately, Saliva began breaking down the food with its special powers as the Tongue tasted the morsels of food.

"Once the food was crushed and broken down, it embarked on its journey down the Esophagus, a long, winding road guarded by the peristaltic waves. With their rhythmic movements, these waves gently guided the food along the path, like a ship sailing on a calm sea, ensuring it reached its next destination safely.

"At the end of the Esophagus lay the grand Stomach. Here, the food was welcomed into the Stomach's great castle, where King Acid's powerful potions and Queen Enzyme's intricate spells worked their magic. They broke the food down even further, transforming it into a magical mixture called chyme. This chyme, a product of the Stomach's enchanting alchemy, was now ready for the next leg of its journey.

"Leaving the Stomach, the chyme entered the Small Intestine, a place of remarkable transformation. The wise Pancreas and the nurturing Liver came to the chyme's aid in this tiny kingdom. The Pancreas provided a bounty of enzymes, each one a key to unlocking essential nutrients. Meanwhile, the Liver sent her loyal bile soldiers to help break down fats, making it easier for the body to absorb them. They also came to clean the blood and store energy in sugar called glycogen. The Small Intestine was lined with tiny villi trees, whose branches reached out to absorb the nutrients, sending them into the bloodstream to nourish the entire big kingdom.

"As the journey neared its end, the remaining chyme entered the Large Intestine, a place of final preparation. Here, the Water Guardians worked diligently to absorb any remaining water, turning the chyme into a more solid form. The friendly bacteria Microbiota also resided here, aiding in the final stages of digestion, and producing essential vitamins for the human kingdom.

"Finally, the now-formed waste reached the Rectal Gate, the exit of the GI Realm. With a gentle push, the waste, called feces or poop, was sent out into the world, completing its long and transformative journey."

The End

"Mrs. Crudlen, I liked that touch of fantasy," I said.

"Good," she responded, "now let us bite into the details, chew them up, and digest them.

"The brain and the gastrointestinal system are intimately connected. The brain uses motor neurons to coordinate the muscles that open and close the jaws, which produce chewing, and it sends messages to the digestive glands, such as the liver. The teeth bite, tear, and slice food, crush it, and grind it. Then, the thousand taste buds that taste the chemicals sweet, salty, sour, or bitter in food begin working. Taste buds are mainly on the tongue, but many others are inside the oral cavity. It helps your digestive system if you take time to chew, chew, chew, and bite, bite, bite your food.

"Saliva, or spit, is around 99% water, plus electrolytes, mucus, white blood cells, epithelial cells, enzymes, and antimicrobial agents. Saliva is produced by three pairs of major salivary glands and hundreds of minor salivary glands. Saliva contains the enzyme amylase, which begins breaking down carbohydrates into simpler sugars. It also contains lysozyme, which breaks down bacteria, preventing overgrowth in your mouth. The salivary glands produce about 32 ounces of saliva every day. That's enough for a fun spittin' contest!

"The chewed food, now called a bolus, is pushed to the back of the throat by your tongue and enters the esophagus. It takes about 10 seconds for food to reach your stomach. The esophagus is a strong, muscular tube that connects the throat with the stomach. It is approximately 11 inches long and is lined with mucous membranes to help with the passage of food and liquids. Peristalsis is a series of coordinated wave-like muscle contractions that help push food down the esophagus and into the stomach. The esophagus has two sphincters. Sphincters are ring-shaped muscles that open and close by relaxing or tightening. The upper sphincter at the top controls the passage of food from the mouth to the esophagus. The lower esophageal sphincter at the bottom prevents stomach contents from flowing back into the esophagus.

"The stomach is a muscular, stretchy organ located in the upper abdomen and attached to the esophagus's end and the small intestine's beginning. It is shaped like a pear and acts like a large mixer. It can hold up to 4 pounds of food at once or about 1.5 liters of food and liquid. The stomach also helps kill bacteria that may be present in food. The pyloric sphincter at the bottom of the stomach governs the passage of food into the small intestines.

"The stomach's leading digestive juice is hydrochloric acid, which can be highly corrosive. To protect itself, the stomach has a thick layer of mucus that prevents the acid from digesting the stomach itself. The stomach muscles churn and mix the food with digestive juices with acids and enzymes, breaking it into much smaller, digestible pieces. Next, the food becomes a semi-liquid mixture called chyme. This mixture is slowly released into the small intestine for further digestion and absorption of nutrients.

"The duodenum is the first section of the small intestine located just below the stomach. It plays a crucial role by receiving partially digested food from the stomach and mixing it with digestive enzymes from the pancreas and bile from the liver and gallbladder. This helps further break down the food so nutrients can be absorbed efficiently.

"The pancreas, gallbladder, and liver play crucial roles in the digestive system.

"The liver is located in the upper right side of the abdomen. It is responsible for many functions that help support metabolism, immunity, digestion, detoxification, and vitamin storage. It also detoxifies the blood by removing toxins and produces proteins necessary for blood clotting. It weighs about three pounds in an adult and is almost six inches long.

"The gallbladder is a small pear-shaped organ located under the liver. The average gallbladder is 3-4 inches long and 2 inches wide at the widest point. It primarily functions as a storage organ for bile produced by the liver. Bile helps break down fats in the small intestine.

"When food containing fat enters the small intestine, a hormone signals the gallbladder to contract and release bile into the digestive system. Bile ducts carry bile from the liver to the gallbladder for storage or to the small intestines. Bile aids in the digestion and absorption of fats by breaking them down into smaller particles that can be easily digested. The liver and gallbladder work harmoniously to ensure proper digestion and nutrient absorption in the body.

"The pancreas is situated behind the stomach. It is about 6 inches long and almost 2 inches wide. It aids digestion by producing enzymes that break down carbohydrates, proteins, and fats in the small intestine. It also regulates blood sugar levels by secreting insulin and glucagon. Insulin is needed to move glucose into cells for energy and storage. Glucagon treats low blood sugar.

"Cells lining your stomach and small intestine make and release hormones that tell your body when to make digestive juices and signal to your brain that you are hungry or full.

"The jejunum and ilium are the middle and final sections of the small intestine where enzymes and bile continue working, and nutrient absorption primarily occurs. The inner walls of the small intestine are lined with villi and microvilli, which are finger-like projections that increase the surface area for absorption. Your small intestines are about 17 feet long.

"The large intestine is about 5 feet long. The large intestine absorbs water and electrolytes from the remaining indigestible food matter. As water is absorbed, the waste material solidifies into feces or stool. Beneficial bacteria in the colon continue to break down any remaining nutrients, producing gases and additional beneficial compounds that aid in vitamin production and fermentation. The rectum stores feces until defecation or pooping. When the rectum is full, stretch receptors signal the brain, triggering the urge to defecate, which is discharging feces from the body. The anal sphincters relax, allowing feces to be expelled through the anus. The odor of feces is caused by bacteria and the process of breaking down food. Usually, food takes 24 to 72 hours to pass through the digestive system.

"A burp, belch, or eructate is the release of gas from the stomach through the mouth. It is typically caused by swallowing air while eating or drinking, drinking carbonated beverages, or eating too quickly. On the other hand, flatulence, passing gas, occurs when gas accumulates in the digestive system and is released through the rectum. Some people call it farting. This gas can be produced by digesting certain foods and swallowing air. Both eructation and flatulence are natural bodily functions that help release excess gas and relieve discomfort. A growling stomach is caused by peristalsis, the contraction of muscles in the stomach and intestines to help move food and gas through the digestive system. When the stomach is empty, the muscles contract, creating the rumbling or growling sound we hear. Other causes of a growling stomach can include increased stomach acid production, gas, air moving through the intestines, or food intolerances.

"Beneficial bacteria are primarily located in the ileum in the small intestine and cecum in the large intestine where partially digested food gets blended with your body's bacteria before moving on.

"Good bacteria in the gut, also known as probiotics, play a crucial role in maintaining a healthy digestive system. Our gut is home to trillions of bacteria, called microorganisms or microbes. This is a vast community of microorganisms, including beneficial and harmful bacteria. 85% of bacteria species are beneficial to our health. Beneficial bacteria help with digestion, absorption of nutrients, and support the immune system. They also help in preventing the growth of harmful bacteria by maintaining a balanced gut microbiome. A microbiome is a community of microorganisms that exist in a particular environment, like the GI tract. Their presence not only enhances nutrient absorption but also contributes to a balanced mood and robust immune response, showcasing the benefits of a healthy gut microbiome. On the other hand, bad bacteria in the gut, also known as pathogens, can disturb the balance of the gut microbiome.

"When harmful bacteria overpower good bacteria, it can result in digestive problems and even chronic diseases. Some can be toxic and cause infections that lead to inflammation of the gut lining. This can damage the cells lining the gut, impair nutrient absorption, and trigger immune responses.

"Gut microbes produce or help produce many of the chemical neurotransmitters that send messages between the gut and brain. Gut bacteria may influence emotions and cognitive abilities. Good bacteria in our digestive tract play a crucial role in maintaining our overall health. However, as we age, so does the wonderful ecosystem in our gut. So, eat more veggies!

"I am finished, Mimi. Do you want to say anything?"

"Yes ma'am. I want to add that Hippocrates, the ancient Greek physician known as the 'Father of Medicine' believed that a healthy diet played a crucial role in maintaining overall well-being and preventing illness. Hippocrates lived during the Classical Greek period, and he died in 370 B.C. at the age of 90. He emphasized the importance of food as medicine, famously stating, 'Let food be thy medicine and medicine be thy food.'"

CHAPTER 13
The Lymphatic System

Imagine the moment before a big introduction, where anticipation fills the air and suddenly, Mrs. Crudlen declares, "Drum Roll!" Next, she rapidly moved her hands doing a pretend drum roll, flicking her tongue back and forth against the roof of her mouth, creating a continuous "trrrr" sound. Next, the sounds became longer and louder "Trrrrrrrrrrrr! Trrrrrrrrrrrrrrrrr!" Then Mrs. Crudlen proudly announced—the miraculous Lymphatic System!

The drum roll added a theatrical flair to the introduction. I wondered why the drama, and as if she knew what I was thinking, she replied, "Mimi, I wanted to create a memorable introduction for the lymphatic system because it is vital to the immune system. Immune means resistant to disease in common medical talk. The lymphatic system cleans, drains, and defends the body, which saves lives. The lymphatic system is not listed as a separate body system in many recent educational information. However, I am from the old school and want to give my overview of this fascinating system."

Mrs. Crudlen leaned forward as she began, her voice clear and deliberate. "Mimi, think of the lymphatic system as the body's unsung hero. The lymphatic system runs through the body like a drainage system. It creates a network of branches covering most of the body tissues. It comprises tiny tubes called lymph vessels, filters called lymph nodes, and particular lymphatic organs. Lymph, the clear fluid containing white blood cells, flows through the lymphatic system. Lymph comes from body tissues and drains into small lymphatic vessels all over the body. From there, it connects with lymphatic ducts in the upper chest, which are large channels that return lymph back into the bloodstream. Lymphatic ducts help maintain fluid balance, immune function, and fat absorption."

Mrs. Crudlen paused, and her eyes began to sparkle. "I just thought of a good idea, Mimi. You ask me some good questions about the lymphatic system, and I will give you some answers. Do you want to?"

"Yes, ma'am. I like that idea. Here goes! What are lymph nodes?"

"Lymph nodes filter the lymph. They are small, bean-shaped structures that trap and destroy germs and other harmful stuff before they can spread in the body. Our bodies have about 600 to 700 lymph nodes, but you only feel them when they are swollen from fighting the bad guys. They're mainly clustered in your neck, armpits, and groin, but you have them all over."

"I didn't realize there were that many! It's amazing how much goes on inside our bodies." I paused and thought of another question. "What makes the lymphatic system move through the body?"

"The lymphatic system doesn't have a central pump like the heart, so it relies on movement, muscle contractions, and breathing," Mrs. Crudlen explained. "Lymphatic vessels contain walls and valves that regulate the flow of lymph. These valves keep it from flowing backward, guiding it toward the lymph nodes and eventually back into the bloodstream. When you move, breathe, or even stretch, your muscles squeeze the lymph vessels, pushing the fluid along. It collects things your body does not need—like bacteria, viruses, and waste—and moves them toward lymph nodes, which filter and destroy them. After filtering, the lymphatic vessels eventually merge into larger vessels that empty into the bloodstream, returning the lymph to circulation. This helps maintain a fluid balance in the body by collecting excess fluid from tissues and returning it to the bloodstream. This process prevents tissue swelling, called edema.

"Lymph nodes are packed with immune cells—B cells and T cells— that detect and attack anything harmful."

I leaned closer. "B cells and T cells—what exactly do they do?"

Her response was quick. "B cells produce antibodies, which latch onto invaders like viruses and bacteria, marking them for destruction. T cells directly attack infected or abnormal cells. The lymph nodes are like their command centers where they coordinate their attack."

"How clever! And where do these B and T cells come from?"

I could tell Mrs. Crudlen liked my questions. Her face lit up with enthusiasm when she responded. "They are born in the bone marrow, that spongy tissue inside our bones. The bone marrow creates B and T cells. B cells mature in the marrow, while T cells take a detour to the thymus gland, located just behind the breastbone, the sternum. It trains and matures the T cells to recognize foreign antigens but not attack the body's tissues. An antigen is a substance that causes the body to make an immune response against that substance."

Suddenly, I realized I was secretly challenging her with my questions, which was fun. I asked quickly. "And what about the spleen? What does it do?" I grinned and nodded.

Mrs. Crudlen gave me a piercing stare that seemed to cut through the air like a sharpened blade, conveying a silent message of disapproval that needed no words.

I felt a tinge of guilt creep in as I grappled with the consequences of my challenging her. "I took a deep breath, let it out, and said, "I'm sorry, I'll slow down the questions."

"No problem…on to the spleen. It is located in the upper left of the abdomen, under the ribcage, and behind the stomach. It filters the blood by removing old or damaged red blood cells, stores platelets, and helps the body fight infections. Additionally, the spleen produces antibodies and stores blood during emergencies, such as excessive bleeding, injury, or stress. You can live without your spleen because the liver can take over many of its functions."

Feeling relaxed again, I leaned back. "So, what about the tonsils and adenoids?"

"Those tissues are part of the first line of defense. Tonsils are located at the back of the throat, while adenoids are situated at the back of the nasal cavity. Both structures comprise lymphoid tissue containing immune cells that help fight off infections. The tonsils function as the first line of defense against pathogens that enter the body through the mouth and nose. They produce antibodies to neutralize harmful bacteria and viruses. Adenoids, on the other hand, help to trap and eliminate germs that are inhaled through the nose. They are like sentinels guarding the entry points to the body."

"What about the Thymus Gland?"

"Mimi, I discussed the thymus gland earlier. The thymus gland is a small, irregular-shaped organ in the upper chest, between the lungs, and behind the breastbone, the sternum. It is part of the lymphatic and endocrine systems. It primarily produces and matures white blood cells called T lymphocytes, which fight infections. It identifies and destroys cancer cells and pathogens. It recognizes which viruses and bacteria to attack in the future. It also produces hormones. The thymus gland grows to its largest size during childhood and makes all the T cells we need before we become teenagers. After this, it gradually gets smaller and becomes less active."

"Is the appendix part of the lymphatic system?"

"Yes. The appendix is a small pouch-like organ located at the end of the large intestine, typically in the lower right abdomen. It is usually about 3.5 inches to 4 inches long, but its size can vary from person to person. The exact function of the appendix is still somewhat of a mystery, but it is believed to play a role in the immune system as it contains lymphatic tissue that helps fight off infections. In some cases, the appendix can become inflamed and infected, a condition known as appendicitis, which may require surgical removal to prevent complications."

"And the Peyer's patches?" I asked with excitement.

"Ah, the Peyer's patches," she said with a grin. "They are small lymphoid tissues in your intestines. They are found in the small intestine lining and help protect the body against harmful bacteria and pathogens that may enter the digestive tract. Overall, Peyer's patches in the gut help to prevent the spread of infections and maintain the balance between our immune system and the trillions of microbes living in our digestive tract.

"And speaking of the digestive tract. Lacteals are specialized lymphatic vessels in the small intestine that play a crucial role in absorbing dietary fats and fat-soluble vitamins. These unique vessels are lined with cells that increase surface area and are responsible for transporting nutrients from the digestive system to the bloodstream. Lacteals are essential for the overall function of the lymphatic system by helping to maintain fluid balance, immune response, and nutrient absorption."

"This is fascinating!" I sat back, beaming with pride, thinking about the lymphatic system. "Mrs. Crudlen, the lymphatic system is intricate and brilliant."

Mrs. Crudlen smiled. "I am glad you enjoyed it, Mimi. I enjoyed your questions."

She quickly moved her hands, doing a pretend drum roll. She flicked her tongue back and forth against the roof of her mouth, creating the "Trrrrrrrrrrr! Trrrrrrrrrrrrrrr!" sound.

CHAPTER 14
Endocrine System

"Hi, Mimi. The Endocrine System is a miraculous, complex system. It is like a messaging system in the body that uses glands and hormones to communicate and regulate different functions. Glands are organs that produce and release chemical messengers called hormones, which travel through the bloodstream to target cells or organs to help them control how they do their work. For example, insulin is a hormone made in the pancreas that regulates how the cells in the body use glucose for energy. Each gland in the endocrine system produces specific hormones that have different roles in the body.

"Now it is time to meet the glands of the endocrine system," Mrs. Crudlen said.

"I would love to meet them. Where are they?"

"At the exciting Gland Land inside the body. Use your prefrontal cortex, parietal lobe, and temporal lobe in your brain to fuel your imagination and let us go."

We were soon at Gland Land. Nestled inside the human body, this special land had a warm and welcoming atmosphere. Each gland was anthropomorphized, looking like a unique character reflecting their function and personality. They gathered around a large table, eager to introduce themselves.

Hypothalamus: An elegant figure, wearing a tailored suit and holding a clipboard. "Hello, guests! I'm the Hypothalamus. I reside in the brain, just above the pituitary gland, in the undersurface of the brain. I am the size of a pea. I am like the command center, which regulates and coordinates activities in different parts of the body. I connect the endocrine system with the nervous system. I release hormones that control the pituitary gland. I keep the body in a stable, constant condition, called homeostasis. I act as the control center for the various processes, like body temperature, hunger, thirst, and sleep. Nice to meet you, nice ladies!"

Pituitary Gland: A small but authoritative figure, dressed in a doctor's white lab coat. "Hi there! I am the Pituitary Gland, often referred to as the 'master gland.' I live right below the hypothalamus in my brain. I use information from the brain to tell other glands in the body what to do. I release hormones that influence growth, reproductive functions, and metabolism, which manage and transfer energy from food. I act based on the commands from my boss, the incredible hypothalamus. Pleased to make your acquaintance!"

Thyroid Gland: A graceful figure, adorned with a necklace resembling a butterfly. "Greetings! I am the thyroid gland in the neck, wrapped around the windpipe. I produce hormones that regulate metabolism, energy levels, and overall growth and development. I'm all about keeping the energy balanced."

Parathyroid Glands: Four tiny figures wearing identical straw hats, always together, speaking harmoniously. "Hello! We are the Parathyroid Glands, residing right behind the thyroid gland in the neck. We produce parathyroid hormones, which regulate calcium, magnesium, and phosphorus levels in the bones and blood. We ensure your bones stay strong and your muscles work properly."

Adrenal Glands: Two energetic figures, wearing athletic gear. Each one perched on top of a kidney. "Hey there! We are the Adrenal Glands. We produce cortisol, adrenaline, and aldosterone. Cortisol helps manage stress, metabolism, oxygen intake, blood flow, and sexual function. Adrenaline gives you that 'fight or flight' energy boost, and aldosterone controls blood pressure by managing sodium and water balance. We are all about keeping you ready for action!"

Pancreas: A gentle, wise figure wearing a chef's hat. "Hello, ladies! I am the Pancreas, nestled in the abdomen behind the stomach. I have a dual role, endocrine and digestive. My endocrine part produces insulin and glucagon to regulate blood sugar levels, ensuring you have the right amount of sugar in your bloodstream and your cells for energy. My exocrine part helps with digestion by producing enzymes that make protein. Balance and nourishment are my main concerns."

Ovaries: Two elegant figures, wearing floral crowns. "Hi! We are the Ovaries, located in the lower abdomen on either side of the uterus in females. We produce estrogen and progesterone, which regulate the menstrual cycle, pregnancy, and secondary sexual characteristics. We're all about fertility and femininity."

Testes: Two robust figures, with a sporty look. "Hey! We are the Testes, found in the scrotum in males. We produce testosterone, which is crucial for sperm production, muscle mass, and male secondary sexual characteristics. We help grow facial and body hair at puberty. Strength and virility are our domains."

Pineal: A delicate figure wearing a traditional habit that consists of a long, loose-fitting tunic, white cap, and veil. "Blessings. I am a small gland located in the brain near the center, between the two hemispheres. I produce melatonin, a hormone that helps regulate sleep-wake cycles and is influenced by the amount of light received through the eyes. I am also associated with spiritual experiences and have long been a subject of fascination and study in both scientific and philosophical circles."

Thalamus: A stout figure wearing a hat and uniform that is highly visible, designed for safety and authority. "Hello! I am a small, walnut-shaped structure located in the brain's center, positioned above the hypothalamus and below the cerebral cortex. I act as a crucial relay station, receiving sensory and motor signals and then transmitting them to the appropriate areas of the cerebral cortex. In addition to sensory functions, I also play a role in regulating consciousness, sleep, and alertness."

The characters chatted animatedly, sharing stories of how their ductless glands work together to keep the body in balance while using the bloodstream to communicate with each other and the nervous system. They mentioned their system's two types of glands: endocrine and exocrine glands. In simple terms, endocrine glands release hormones into the bloodstream to communicate with various parts of the body. An exocrine gland releases substances through ducts or openings to the body's surface to perform specific functions locally, such as sweat, tears, or saliva.

The hypothalamus, as the unofficial leader, ensured us everyone was in sync, highlighting the interconnectedness of the endocrine system. After a nudge from the pituitary gland, the hypothalamus thanked Mrs. Crudlen for the invitation and wonderful socialization, told us goodbye, and each one returned where they came from.

CHAPTER 15
Nervous System

"The miraculous nervous system is a complex network of nerves and cells that transmit signals between different parts of the body. It is a communication network that uses electrical and chemical means to send and receive messages. It is divided into two main parts: the central nervous system, which includes the brain, spinal cord, and nerves, and the peripheral nervous system, which consists of all the nerves outside the central nervous system. It allows different body parts to work together by coordinating everything we do, such as movement, sensation, thought, and regulation of internal organs. We need the nervous system to think, move, and breathe.

"The brain is my favorite organ in the body!" Mrs. Crudlen exclaimed. "It is the command center of our body." She grinned and added, "I like the names of brain parts; they sound like pretty words to me.

"Your brain is fragile; it weighs about 3 pounds and has about 100 billion neurons. Neurons are also called nerves. Imagine neurons as the brain's tiny messengers. Neurons are the basic building blocks of the brain and nervous system. Neurons carry signals to and from the brain. They are specialized cells that transmit information through electrical and chemical signals. Neurons have a cell body with branching extensions called dendrites and an elongated projection called an axon. They are like highways that allow information to travel quickly throughout the body. Synapses are the connections between neurons where signals are passed from one cell to another. They are like bridges that allow communication between neurons. At the synapse, electrical signals are converted into chemical signals that travel across a small gap called the synaptic cleft. This transmission of signals is crucial for functions like thinking, feeling, and moving. Neurons, also called nerves, and synapses in the brain work together to process information and coordinate the body's activities.

"The autonomic nervous system is like the autopilot of our body, controlling involuntary functions such as heart rate and digestion. It has two main branches: the sympathetic system, which speeds up our fight-or-flight responses, and the parasympathetic nervous system, which helps us rest and digest. The peripheral nervous system connects the central nervous system to the rest of the body. It is responsible for transmitting information between the brain and the rest of the body. It comprises cranial, spinal, and peripheral nerves, which transmit sensory information and conduct motor commands.

"The skull does a fantastic job of protecting the brain.

"The brain can be divided into parts and regions, each with specific functions and locations. The Cerebrum is the largest part of the brain. It is responsible for thinking, sensory perception, and voluntary movement. It is divided into two hemispheres, the right and left side of the brain, connected by a bundle of nerve fibers called the corpus callosum. The right side of the brain is associated with creativity, intuition, and spatial awareness, while the left side is known for logic, language, and analytical thinking. Each hemisphere controls the opposite side of the body, with the right hemisphere controlling the left side and the left hemisphere controlling the right side."

Mrs. Crudlen paused, drank water, and said, "Now, I will introduce brain parts as if they were celebrities. Mimi, please listen actively and prepare yourselves for a spectacular time as I introduce some of the most iconic figures in the brain's celebrity lineup. Each of these illustrious stars plays a unique and crucial role in the grand performance that is in your body!

"First on the red carpet, we have the Amygdala! The Drama Queen. Known for her intense emotional performances, the Amygdala is the heart and soul of our emotional experiences. Whether it is fear, anger, or joy, she brings the drama and ensures we feel every moment deeply. There are two located in the temporal lobes above each ear. The two are considered one brain area and part of the limbic system.

"Next, the Pineal Gland steps into the spotlight! The Timekeeper. Small but mighty, the Pineal Gland is our master of ceremonies for the sleep-wake cycle. Producing melatonin, he ensures we stay on schedule, balancing our circadian rhythms and helping us get a good night's sleep. The pineal gland is located deep within the brain, in a small, pea-sized gland at the center of the brain, near the hypothalamus, and just above the brainstem. It has been called 'The Third Eye' and is associated with spirituality.

"Now, let us welcome Hippocampus! The Memory Maestro. With an incredible talent for storytelling, the Hippocampus is our memory's guardian. He helps us remember the past and learn new things, making sure our life's story is always rich and detailed. Two hippocampi are small horse-shaped structures located in the brain's medial temporal lobe, deep in the skull near the ears and temples. Additionally, research suggests that the hippocampus regulates emotions and stress responses.

"Making her grand entrance, it is the Thalamus! The Sensory Gatekeeper. The Thalamus is the elegant hostess who directs all sensory information to the appropriate places in the brain. Whether it is sight, sound, touch, or taste, but not smell, she ensures everything is processed smoothly and efficiently. It acts as a gateway for sensory data to the cerebral cortex, helping to regulate consciousness, sleep, and alertness. It is egg-shaped and located deep within the brain, above the brain stem.

"Prepare to be amazed by the Pituitary Gland! The Master Controller, often called the Master Gland, the Pituitary gland is a small pea-sized gland located at the base of the brain, just below the hypothalamus. It is the powerhouse behind our body's hormone production. He controls other hormone-secreting glands in the body, including the thyroid, adrenal glands, and reproductive glands. He helps keep everything in balance, maintaining the body's internal balance, known as homeostasis. He is like a true conductor of the body's orchestra.

"The marvelous Meninges take center stage! The Protective Trio. The Meninges are the ultimate bodyguards, comprising three layers, protecting the brain and spinal cord with unmatched dedication and strength from injury and infection. The dura mater is the tough outer layer, the arachnoid mater is the delicate middle layer, and the pia mater is the thin inner layer that directly covers the brain and spinal cord. The meninges also contain cerebrospinal fluid, which acts as a cushion to absorb impacts and provide nutrients to the brain.

"Gray Matter and White Matter: We have a dynamic duo. Gray and white matter are two types of tissue found in the brain. Gray Matter is the brain's celebrity thinker, packed with neuron cell bodies and responsible for processing information. Always the life of the party, Gray Matter makes sure everything runs smoothly. White Matter, on the other hand, is the ultimate connector, filled with myelinated axons that act like high-speed internet cables, ensuring quick and efficient communication between different brain regions. Gray matter contains cell bodies, dendrites, and axon terminals. White matter consists mostly of axons connecting different brain areas and allowing neurons to communicate.

"Frontal Lobe: Please welcome the multitasking maestro, the Frontal Lobe! This part of the brain is the executive director, overseeing decision-making, problem-solving, memory, and planning. Known for its control over personality and behavior, the Frontal Lobe keeps things organized and in check, ensuring you make smart choices. It also plays a key role in voluntary movement and language production. Two lobes are located in the front of the brain, one on each side behind the forehead.

"Temporal Lobe: Did you hear the one about the temporal lobe? The temporal lobe is responsible for making sense of sounds, understanding what people say, remembering important events, including faces, and feeling emotions like happiness or fear. There are two lobes, and they sit behind the temples on both sides of the brain.

"Parietal Lobe: Let's give it up for the Parietal Lobe, one of the brain's spatial superstars! This lobe is all about sensation and perception. It's not just about touch, temperature, and pain but also about understanding spatial orientation and body awareness. It's the brain's GPS, helping you navigate your environment and feel connected to your body. There are two lobes positioned in the top and back of the brain.

"Occipital Lobe: And now, the visual virtuoso, the Occipital Lobe. This lobe is your go-to for all things visual. It's not just about processing and interpreting everything you see, but it's like the brain's personal cinematographer, making sense of colors, shapes, and movements. Two lobes are found in the back of the brain entertaining us with its cinematic capabilities.

"Cerebellum: Make some noise for the coordination queen! This part of the brain is all about balance, movement, and coordination. The Cerebellum ensures your movements are smooth and precise, whether dancing, playing sports, or simply walking. Think of it as the brain's dance choreographer, ensuring all your movements are smooth and coordinated. It may also have cognitive functions. Three lobes are located at the back of the brain beneath the occipital lobes, entertaining us with their dance moves.

"Hypothalamus: Honor this honorable, small, and powerful man by standing! This part of the brain is crucial in regulating many essential bodily functions. It is located deep within the brain, above the brain stem, and below the thalamus. It acts as the control center for various processes like body temperature, hunger, thirst, sleep, and hormonal balance. Essentially, the hypothalamus helps keep your body in harmony and ensures everything is running smoothly to keep you healthy and functioning optimally.

"Gyri and Sulci: These pretty words are the pretty folds on the brain. They are essential for increasing the surface area of the brain within the confined space of the skull. These folds enhance the brain's cognitive abilities by allowing for more neurons and synapses to be packed into a smaller space. The gyri are the raised ridges on the brain's surface, while the sulci are the grooves or furrows between them. Together, they create a complex network that enables communication between the brain, facilitating various functions such as sensory processing, motor coordination, and higher cognitive processes.

"Brain Stem: Next, let us show some love for the Brain Stem, the brain's essential worker! The Brain Stem is the powerhouse that controls basic life functions such as breathing, heart rate, and blood pressure. It keeps you alive and well, working tirelessly behind the scenes. It is located at the bottom of the brain at the back of the skull. It is a tube-shaped mass of nervous tissue a little over three inches long. The brain stem includes the Pons, which helps control our breathing, and the Medulla Oblongata, which regulates our heart and reflexes like vomiting, coughing, and swallowing.

"Brain ventricles are small cavities in the brain filled with cerebrospinal fluid, which helps protect the brain and spinal cord. There are four ventricles in total, and they are phenomenal! They provide nutrients, remove waste, help regulate intracranial pressure, and support the surrounding structures.

"Don't forget The Limbic System. The limbic system is a complex network of various brain regions that regulate emotions, behavior, motivation, and memory. It comprises several vital structures, including the amygdala, hippocampus, thalamus, hypothalamus, and cingulate gyrus. The cingulate gyrus also plays a role in attention and emotional processing. It is located deep within the cerebral hemispheres.

"Spinal Cord: A special shoutout to the Spinal Cord, the brain's trusted courier! The Spinal Cord is a crucial communication highway, carrying messages between the brain and the rest of the body. It is a thin, tubular bundle of nervous tissue extending from the brain down the spinal column, also called the backbone, spine, and vertebral column. The spinal cord ensures that sensory information and motor commands travel back and forth efficiently. It can process sensory information to produce a spinal reflex without initiating input from the brain. It is protected by the vertebrae. Cerebrospinal fluid flows in and around the spinal cord to protect it. The spinal cord is vital in relaying messages and coordinating body movements, sensations, and organ function.

"12 pairs of cranial nerves: This darling dozen emerges directly from the brain and brainstem rather than from the spinal cord. They transmit sensory and motor information between the body and the brain. The functions they control are primarily related to the head and neck, including vision, smell, taste, hearing, balance, facial movement, and swallowing. Some nerves carry only sensory information, some only motor, and others a mix of both. Damage or compression to any of these nerves can lead to various neurological problems and impairments.

"Dermatomes will now be acknowledged for their helpful specific skin areas with sensory nerves from a single spinal nerve root. These nerve roots transmit sensations such as pain, temperature, touch, and pressure from the skin to the brain. By mapping out the dermatomes on the body, healthcare professionals can pinpoint the location of nerve damage or dysfunction.

"So, there you have it, an all-star lineup! They are true celebrities, each contributing to the grand symphony that is the human experience. Each part plays a unique and vital role in keeping you thinking, feeling, moving, and living your best life. Mimi, give them a round of applause!"

I gave the celebrities a standing ovation, clapped and clapped, and said, "Mrs. Crudlen, I'm so grateful to you for every word you said about the nervous system."

"Mimi, gratitude activates regions of the brain associated with dopamine production. Dopamine is a neurotransmitter produced in the brain that plays a key role in reward-motivated behavior, making us happy and satisfied. The act of feeling grateful can increase the production of serotonin, another neurotransmitter associated with feelings of well-being and happiness. Expressing gratitude has been shown to lower levels of cortisol, promoting a sense of calm and relaxation. Gratitude can activate the parasympathetic nervous system. This activation can lead to lower heart rates, improved digestion, and a general state of relaxation. Positive emotions like gratitude can enhance immune function. People who practice gratitude tend to have better sleep quality."

I smiled a great big smile, expressing my gratitude as Mrs. Crudlen continued talking.

"It is time to talk about other parts of the nervous system — hearing, smelling, and vision. The eye is an extraordinarily complex organ responsible for vision in the human body. It is composed of several structures that work together to capture and process visual information. Its structure includes the cornea, iris, pupil, lens, retina, and optic nerve. Light enters through the cornea and passes through the pupil, which adjusts in size and is controlled by the iris. The lens focuses the light onto the retina, which contains photoreceptor cells called rods and cones that convert light into electrical signals. These signals are sent through the optic nerve to the brain for processing and interpretation, resulting in the perception of images and visual information. The eye's ability to refract light, focus images, and convert light into signals makes it essential for sight and visual perception.

"The ear is another complex organ responsible for hearing and balance. It consists of three main parts: the outer ear, middle ear, and inner ear. The outer ear includes the visible part known as the pinna. The earlobe is the lower soft part of the pinna. The pinna collects sound waves that go through the ear canal to the eardrum in the middle ear. The ear canal is lined with hair follicles and glands that produce ear wax. Ear wax helps protect the ear canal. The middle ear contains three tiny bones, the hammer, anvil, and stirrup, called ossicles, that amplify and transmit sound vibrations to the inner ear. The inner ear contains the cochlea, a spiral-shaped structure filled with fluid and hair cells that convert sound waves into electrical signals sent to the brain for interpretation. Additionally, the inner ear houses the semicircular canals, which help us maintain our sense of balance.

"The nose is a prominent facial feature that serves as the primary organ for the sense of smell. It is made up of bone, cartilage, and soft tissue, with two nostrils for breathing and detecting smells. The main functions of the nose include filtering, warming, and humidifying the air we breathe before it reaches the lungs. The nose also plays a crucial role in our sense of taste by helping to enhance and identify different flavors in food. When we eat, aroma compounds from the food travel up to the back of the nose through the passage that connects the mouth and the nose. These compounds interact with the olfactory receptors in the nose, sending signals to the brain that help us distinguish between various tastes. There are 400 types of receptors to pick up odors and send them to the brain. When we have a stuffy nose or a cold, our ability to taste food is greatly reduced because the aroma cannot reach the olfactory receptors effectively. Another function of the nose is to produce mucus to trap harmful particles and prevent them from entering the respiratory system.

"Dreams are mysterious and complex phenomena that have fascinated humans for centuries. The question of where dreams come from is still not fully understood, but they are believed to originate in the brain during the rapid eye movement stage of sleep. While some people believe that dreams have deep symbolic meanings and can offer insights into our subconscious minds, others view them as simply a result of random brain activity. In terms of the brain, dreams are thought to involve various parts of the brain, including the prefrontal cortex, which is responsible for decision-making and emotions, and the amygdala, which engages in processing emotions and memories. More research is needed to fully understand the origins and significance of dreams.

"Rapid Eye Movement plays a vital role in the sleep cycle. During REM sleep, the body is immobilized to prevent sleepwalking, while the brain is highly active, processing memories and emotions. This stage repeats multiple times throughout the night. REM sleep is crucial for cognitive functions, mood regulation, and overall well-being. Prioritizing high-quality sleep and ensuring an adequate amount of time in the REM stage can lead to improved mental and physical health.

"The conscious mind is the part of our mental processing that we are aware of, including our thoughts, perceptions, and memories that we actively think about. It is located in the frontal lobe of the brain, which is responsible for decision-making and problem-solving. On the other hand, the subconscious mind operates below the level of conscious awareness, influencing our behavior, emotions, and beliefs without us realizing it. The subconscious mind is spread out throughout the brain, with areas such as the amygdala and hippocampus playing key roles in processing emotions and memories. These two aspects of the mind work together to shape our perceptions and actions, with the subconscious mind often influencing our conscious thoughts and behaviors without us realizing it."

As soon as I finished my conscious thoughts about what she said, Mrs. Crudlen told me some fascinating brain features. And here they are!

1. Your nerve impulses travel at speeds of up to 250 miles per hour.
2. Your brain generates enough electricity to power a light bulb.
3. Your brain can store data equivalent to about 3 million hours of TV shows.
4. Your brain generates about 70,000 thoughts per day.
5. Your nervous system can adapt and change throughout life, a process known as neuroplasticity. You can develop new skills, memories, and mindsets! Go for it!

"Mimi, I would like to add one more fascinating fact. According to the American Association of Retired Persons, AARP, in a groundbreaking report, experts concluded that listening to and making music holds significant potential to support our brain health!"

Next, she stood, reached behind her back, and pulled out a small-brimmed, sleek black hat. She placed it on her head and tilted it forward ever so slightly, adding an air of mystery to her look.

The mystery was soon solved when she started singing *Ease on Down the Road.*

"Come on, ease on down, ease on down the road
Come on, ease on down, ease on down the road
Don't you carry nothin' that might be a load
Come on, ease on down, ease on down, down the road."

I could feel the rhythm pulsating into my brain, listening to the iconic song with its upbeat and infectious tempo. Move over Diana Ross! Then, Mrs. Crudlen started dancing Micheal Jackson's legendary moonwalk dance while she sang! Gliding effortlessly across the porch, she defied gravity with her backward quick steps, and smooth and precise footwork and spins. The hat perched on her head remained perfectly in place, adding to the illusion of her effortless old lady coolness with mesmerizing dance moves. I grinned an ear-to-ear grin, capturing the sheer magic of the moment as a lasting memory in my hippocampus.

CHAPTER 16
The Integumentary System

"Hello, Mimi! Now, I am going to talk about skin. It is more than just what you see in the mirror; it is a miraculous, complex system called the Integumentary System! And it is our last system to discuss.

"Before we talk about specifics in the Integumentary System, I want to share some interesting information. It is the largest system in the body. The skin of an average adult has a surface area of about 21 square feet. It contains 11 miles of blood vessels. It has approximately 100 oil glands, 650 sweat glands, and 1,000 nerve endings in a square inch. Your skin sheds about 9 pounds of dead skin cells yearly. It makes up twelve to fifteen percent of your body weight.

"The integumentary system is like a superhero suit for your body. It provides a tough, flexible covering for your body. Integumentary means covering in Latin. Your skin prevents pathogens, toxins, and other harmful substances from entering the body. It allows you to feel sensations like hot, cold, and pain, prevents water loss, regulates your body temperature, aids in the excretion of waste products through sweat, and makes Vitamin D when exposed to sunlight.

"The skin has three layers. The thin, top layer is the epidermis; this is the part you can see. It is made mostly of epithelial cells and does not contain any blood vessels or glands. The epidermis regenerates every four to six weeks. Cells at the bottom of the epidermal layer constantly divide to create new cells. These new skin cells gradually move upwards and produce a tough protein called keratin. As the skin cells fill with keratin they die. When the dead cells reach the outside of the skin, a waterproof layer of cells is formed that protects the body. These cells shed over time and are replaced with more cells from below.

"The epidermis also contains melanocytes that make melanin. It is the pigment that gives your skin and hair its color. More melanin means darker skin. Increased exposure to ultraviolet light will also make your skin produce more melanin, which is the reason the sun can give you a tan. The average solar damage takes between 15 and 20 years to show the effects. However, intense solar exposure can cause visible damage even earlier."

She paused and said, "Mimi, I read your book, *A Family's Sacred Secret*, and the dialogue you wrote about skin color was heartwarming and powerful."

"Thank you," I replied.

"You are welcome. Keep writing. Now, let us get back to the skin. The Dermis is the middle layer. This connective tissue makes up almost 90% of the thickness of the skin. The dermis has blood vessels, nerves, hair follicles, sweat glands, and oil glands. Blood and lymph capillaries present in the dermis bring oxygen and nutrients to the skin and remove waste. The blood vessels in the dermis can either dilate to allow more blood to get closer to the surface of the skin to release heat or constrict to keep blood toward the inner body and preserve heat. This keeps the body temperature at a consistent level.

"Skin sensory receptors are located throughout the skin in the dermis and epidermis and play a crucial role in detecting various stimuli such as touch, pressure, and temperature. Some are responsible for sensing pain and signaling potential harm or tissue damage. The sensory receptors send signals to the brain, allowing us to interpret and respond to our environment.

"Hair follicles produce hairs. They are located all over the body, except for the palms of the hands and the soles of the feet. Each hair follicle contains a hair bulb at its base, which is nourished by blood vessels. Hair follicles go through cycles of growth, rest, and shedding. During the growth phase, new hair is produced and pushes out the old hair strand. Hair follicles vary in size and shape depending on the body area and can produce different hair types, such as fine and thick. Hair is made of keratin, a fibrous protein. Hair plays a role in maintaining homeostasis by insulating and protecting your head from the sun. Hair follicles also help regulate body temperature by trapping heat close to the body when the hair stands up, like in chills or goosebumps.

"Sebaceous glands, aka oil glands, are located along the hair follicle and produce a waxy oil called sebum that lubricates and moisturizes the hair and skin. They are all over the human body, except for the palms of the hands and soles of the feet. These glands are found in the greatest concentration on the face and scalp. When sebaceous glands become overactive, they can lead to oily skin and acne.

"Sweat glands are coiled, tube-like projections in the skin that help regulate body temperature through producing sweat and evaporation, which cools the body. Each sweat gland has a duct that reaches up to the skin's surface, allowing sweat to escape. Sweat is mostly water but contains salt, proteins, oils, and other waste products. Bacteria feed on sweat in moist, warm environments like armpits.

"Certain areas of the body, like the armpits, groin, and feet, tend to produce stronger smelling sweat due to the higher concentration of sweat glands in those areas. This abundance of sweat glands in these areas allows for efficient cooling of the body through sweat, especially during times of increased heat or physical activity. Overall, the smell of sweat in humans is a natural and essential bodily function that helps regulate body temperature and remove toxins from the body.

"The Hypodermis, or subcutaneous tissue is the bottom layer of the skin and is used mostly for fat storage. It helps keep your body warm and cushions your organs.

"That finishes the layers of skin. Now, I will talk about the other unique structures.

"Nails are composed of a tough protein called keratin, making them strong and waterproof. They serve to protect the tips of our fingers and toes. Nails grow from the base of the nail. Cuticles are a thin layer of clear, dead skin that forms at the base of a nail or underside of the nail skin. Cuticles create a watertight seal that protects nails from bacteria, dirt, and debris, and helps keep them hydrated as they grow.

"Eyelashes and eyebrows help you avoid getting dust and sweat in your eyes, and hair in your nose helps filter out dust and microorganisms before they can enter your body."

Mrs. Crudlen patted her face and said, "Natural aging is due to genetics and the gradual loss of collagen and elastin in the skin as we age. This results in reduced skin elasticity and firmness, leading to the formation of wrinkles. Factors such as prolonged sun exposure, smoking, poor skincare habits, poor hydration, and environmental pollutants can accelerate the aging process and contribute to the development of wrinkles."

Suddenly, Mrs. Crudlen moved her face in various directions, showcasing a tapestry of wrinkles etched with time. The fine lines and deep creases around her mouth deepened as she tilted her head from side to side. Each movement of her face revealed a different facet of her life's journey, from the laughter lines around her eyes to the pain and suffering lines on her forehead. Suddenly, she stopped moving her face, and I saw a look of peace, love, and wisdom—a portrait of beauty from within that transcended her wrinkles.

I stared at her in amazement.

She looked back at me, smiled, and said, "Your skin has many important and powerful functions. So, to end this Integumentary session, I want to say—Love The Skin You Are In!"

***

"Mimi, our Anatomy and Physiology session is officially over, and I have loved every minute! Thank you so much for asking me to help you! I hope this book will spark a renewed sense of wonder in the everyday miraculous miracles that keep us alive. If the reader takes time and appreciates the extraordinary gift of life—the body —we have accomplished our goal."

"Mrs. Crudlen, thank you so much for helping me. I love being with you, and I will miss you. When can I see you again?"

As the final moment of being with her approached, words seemed insufficient, and tears of appreciation and emptiness trickled down my face. I took in a deep breath, let it out, and asked one more time, "Mrs. Crudlen, when can I see you again?"

"Mimi Mathis, you certainly are a sensitive old lady crybaby. I'm just an acronym that you turned into a ninety-year-old lady to help you write a book! You'll see me when you see me by using the parts of your brain associated with your imagination."

The End